EARLY
CHURCH

DISCOVERY GUIDE

That the World May Know® with Ray Vander Laan

EARLY CHURCH

—— 5 LESSONS ON ——

Becoming a Light in the Darkness

DISCOVERY GUIDE

EXPERIENCE THE BIBLE IN HISTORICAL CONTEXT™
Ray Vander Laan
with Stephen and Amanda Sorenson

ZONDERVAN   **FOCUS ON THE FAMILY**

ZONDERVAN

Early Church Discovery Guide
Copyright © 2000, 2008 by Ray Vander Laan

This title is also available as a Zondervan ebook. Visit www.zondervan.com/ebooks.

Requests for information should be addressed to:
Zondervan, 3900 *Sparks Dr. SE, Grand Rapids, Michigan* 49546

Focus on the Family and the accompanying logo and design are federally registered trademarks of Focus on the Family, 8605 *Explorer Drive, Colorado Springs, Colorado* 80920.

That the World May Know is a trademark of Focus on the Family.

ISBN 978-0-310-87962-6

All maps created by International Mapping.

All artwork is courtesy of Ray Vander Laan unless otherwise indicated.

All Scripture quotations are taken from The Holy Bible, *New International Version®, NIV.®* Copyright © 1973, 1978, 1984 by Biblica, Inc.® Used by permission. All rights reserved worldwide.

Any Internet addresses (websites, blogs, etc.) and telephone numbers in this book are offered as a resource. They are not intended in any way to be or imply an endorsement by Zondervan, nor does Zondervan vouch for the content of these sites and numbers for the life of this book.

*Cover design: Do**More**Good®*
Cover photography: BiblePlaces.com
Interior design: Ben Fetterley, Denise Froehlich

Printed in the United States of America

CONTENTS

INTRODUCTION

Because God speaks to us through the Scriptures, studying them is a rewarding experience. Most of the inspired human authors of the Bible, as well as those to whom the words were originally given, were Jews living in the Ancient Near East. God's words and actions spoke to them with such power, clarity, and purpose that they wrote them down and carefully preserved them as an authoritative body of literature.

God's use of human servants in revealing himself resulted in writings that clearly bear the stamp of time and place. The message of the Scriptures is, of course, eternal and unchanging — but the circumstances and conditions of the people of the Bible are unique to their times. Consequently, we most clearly understand God's truth when we know the cultural context within which he spoke and acted and the perception of the people with whom he communicated. This does not mean that God's revelation is unclear if we don't know the cultural context. Rather, by learning how to think and approach life as Abraham, Moses, Ruth, Esther, and Paul did, modern Christians will deepen their appreciation of God's Word. To fully apply the message of the Bible to our lives, we must enter the world of the Bible and familiarize ourselves with its culture.

That is the purpose of this study. The events and characters of the Bible will be presented in their original settings. Although the DVD segments offer the latest archaeological research, this series is not intended to be a definitive cultural and geographical study of the lands of the Bible. No original scientific discoveries are revealed here. The purpose of this study is to help us better understand God's revealed mission for our lives by enabling us to hear and see his words in their original context.

Understanding the World of the Bible

More than 3,800 years ago, God spoke to his servant Abraham: "Go, walk through the length and breadth of the land, for I am giving it to you" (Genesis 13:17). From the outset, God's choice of a Hebrew nomad to begin his plan of salvation (that is still unfolding) was linked to the selection of a specific land where his redemptive work would begin. The nature of God's covenant relationship with his people demanded a place where their faith could be exercised and displayed to all nations so that the world would know of *Yahweh*, the true and faithful God.

In the Old Testament, God promised to protect and provide for the Hebrews. He began by giving them Canaan — a beautiful, fertile land where he would shower his blessings upon them. To possess this land, however, the Israelites had to live obediently before God. The Hebrew Scriptures repeatedly link Israel's obedience to God to the nation's continued possession of Canaan, just as they link its disobedience to the punishment of exile (Leviticus 18:24 – 28). When the Israelites were exiled from the Promised Land (2 Kings 18:11), they did not experience God's blessings. Only when they possessed the land did they know the fullness of God's promises.

By New Testament times, the Jewish people had been removed from the Promised Land by the Babylonians due to Israel's failure to live obediently before God (Jeremiah 25:4 – 11). The exile lasted seventy years, but its impact upon God's people was astounding. New patterns of worship developed, and scribes and experts in God's law shaped the new commitment to be faithful to him. The prophets predicted the appearance of a Messiah like King David who would revive the kingdom of the Hebrew people. Even the Promised Land itself had changed, becoming home to many groups of people whose religious practices, moral values, and lifestyles conflicted with those of the Jews. Living as God's witnesses took on added difficulty as Greek, Roman, and Samaritan worldviews mingled with that of the Israelites. But the mission of God's people did not change. They were still to live so that *the world may know that our God is the true God*.

The Jewish Gospel in a Greek World

From the beginning, God's plan was to reclaim his world. The Jewish people of the Bible had made God known to many of the nations of the world as people from those nations traveled through Israel. The Assyrian dispersion and the Babylonian exile spread God-fearing Jewish people around the known world. Many of them returned to Jerusalem for the yearly feasts that God had commanded. God had prepared carefully and well for the next stage in his great plan of salvation: his people must now live *so that the world may know* in all the world — not just in one small place.

God's people would reveal him to people in places such as Rome, Athens, and the cities of Roman provinces such as Syria and Macedonia. The most pagan of all provinces, Asia Minor, would become a stronghold for the followers of God and the Messiah Jesus. They would serve him while the nations of the world watched and listened.

The triumph of the Christian faith is nowhere more striking or unexpected than in the Roman province of Asia Minor. Known for immorality in lifestyle and in religious practice, this region became Christian within 150 years of Jesus' ministry in Israel. The early missionary, Paul (Saul in Hebrew), spent a great deal of time here and wrote several letters to the followers of Jesus in this province. Peter wrote his letters to the believers here, and John wrote Revelation (and his letters) to the churches of this province. The effectiveness of the early believers is amazing and raises a host of questions with great implications for our world today. How did Jesus prepare his followers for such a mission? What empowered them? What kind of commitments did they have to make to their mission? What did they do that had such an impact on the people of Asia? Some answers to these questions become clear when we study the biblical stories in the context in which they occurred.

Pliny

One of the most important sources of information about life in Asia Minor at the time of the early church comes from a Roman governor named Pliny. His letters, written to the emperor Trajan (AD 98 - 117) are a fascinating description of the relationship between the early believers and the pagan Gentiles in the province of Asia Minor.

Pliny's work provides helpful insights for understanding the stories and teachings of Scripture. In addition, Pliny provides many insights into the view of the new faith held by the people of his time who were not Christians.

Trajan had appointed Pliny to bring order to the area of Pontus (in Asia Minor) because of riots and unrest due to local corruption. Pliny proceeded to ban all social, political, and religious organizations, which created great suffering for the Christians because they were not considered one of the legal religions. Pliny noted that the "superstition" (Christianity) had spread throughout the province and left ancient temples deserted.

Pliny made it clear that being a Christian was a capital offense, and many were accused and charged. Pliny offered them several chances to renounce their faith and then they were executed. In one letter to Trajan, he asked what should be done to those who renounced their faith. Were they still criminals for their actions while they were members of the sect or was their rejection of Jesus sufficient? Trajan replied by making adherence to Christianity a capital offense, although the believers were not to be sought out.

Our Purpose

Biblical writers assumed that their readers were familiar with the geography of the ancient Near East. Today, unfortunately, many Christians do not have even a basic geographical knowledge of the region. This study is designed to help solve that problem. We will be studying the people and events of the Bible in their geographical and historical contexts. Once we know the who, what, and where of a Bible story, we will be able to understand the why. By deepening our understanding of God's Word, we will be able to strengthen our relationships with him.

Western Christianity tends to spiritualize the faith of the people of the Bible. Modern Christians do not always do justice to God's desire that his people live faithfully for him in specific places, influencing the cultures around them by their words and actions. Instead of seeing the places to which God called his people as crossroads from which to influence the world, we focus on the glorious destination to which we are traveling as we ignore the world around us. We are focused on the destination, not the journey. We have unconsciously separated our walk with God from our responsibility to the world in which he has placed us.

In one sense, our earthly experience is simply preparation for an eternity in the new "Promised Land." Preoccupation with this idea, however, distorts the mission God has set for us. That mission is the same one he gave to the Israelites: to live obediently *within* the world so that through us, *the world may know that our God is the one true God.*

EVERYTHING TO LOSE, NOTHING TO GAIN

A short time after Jesus the Messiah ascended to heaven from the Mount of Olives, his disciples started to proclaim his message to the world. They began in the familiar lands of Galilee and Israel. Then they pressed on to the far reaches of their world — even to Asia Minor (present-day Turkey), the most pagan and immoral province in the Roman Empire.

What gave Jesus' disciples the passion to endure hardship and persecution in order to share his message in places God-fearing Jews from Galilee preferred to avoid? What inspired them to go where they had nothing to gain for their efforts — indeed, where they had everything to lose, even life itself? How had Jesus prepared them to live out his teachings in daily life and proclaim them so boldly? This DVD segment will take us to Korazin, Caesarea Philippi, and the Mount of Olives — three specific locations where Jesus trained and taught his disciples that will provide insight into what motivated the early Christian disciples.

Like other rabbis of his day, Jesus interpreted the Torah and taught people to apply its teachings so that they could learn how to obey God. But a rabbi was more than a teacher; a rabbi was a living example of how to live life in the way God intended. So a Jewish disciple (*talmid* in Hebrew) desired not only to learn what the rabbi knew but to act as he acted and to take on the godly character he possessed.

As *talmidim*, Jesus' disciples had a passionate commitment to be like Jesus in every way possible. They not only taught his interpretation of the Torah, they demonstrated to others how to obey God and live in a way that honored him. Wherever they went, they followed Jesus' example and taught in word pictures, using concrete illustrations of familiar objects that helped their listeners understand the message of the kingdom of God. In stark contrast to the disciples of Greek teachers who were trained to stand alone and be self-sufficient in their own knowledge, Jesus' disciples established nurturing communities of believers who supported, encouraged, and — when necessary — corrected one another as they sought to obey God and live out their faith.

The message Jesus gave his disciples to share was also fueled by their passion and commitment. Just days before his crucifixion, Jesus took his disciples to Caesarea Philippi, a stronghold of pagan worship located at the foot of Mount Hermon. Here, a river of spring-fed water rushed out from a deep cave at the base of a rock cliff more than one hundred feet high. This cave, called "the gates of Hades," was believed to be the entrance to the underworld from which the goat-god Pan returned annually to bring fertility to the earth.

In this seemingly strange location, Jesus had three key lessons for his disciples. The first had to do with their answer to Jesus' question, "Who am I?" Jesus knew his disciples would soon go into places where people worshiped Roman emperors and numerous pagan gods. They would need to remember with certainty that Jesus was the *living* Messiah.

The second lesson had to do with the "gates of Hades" and the shrines built into the rock cliff at Caesarea Philippi. This pagan worship center represented everything that was disgusting and wrong with the world, yet Jesus wanted his disciples to build his church on top of that rock. He wanted them to replace the pagan values of the culture with his values. In order to do that, his disciples needed to know that nothing they'd encounter in Asia Minor or anywhere else — even the "gates of Hades" itself — could stand against his power.

The third lesson had to do with Jesus' challenge to follow him. He challenged his disciples and the pagan crowd to give up trying to gain meaning, purpose, significance, and value from life and instead to give their lives to other people as he would. He challenged them to never be ashamed of him or his words. Jesus' boldness in teaching them while they were surrounded by pagan worshipers in

Caesarea Philippi must have given the disciples courage when they later spoke to hostile kings, priests, and Gentiles in palaces, temples, theaters, and arenas.

After his resurrection, Jesus took his disciples to the Mount of Olives for a final lesson. He commanded them to be his witnesses "in Jerusalem, and in all Judea, and Samaria, and to the ends of the earth." Then, he raised his hands to bless them and ascended to heaven while they watched. Within a few years, the Roman emperors' claims to divinity would erupt into widespread emperor worship. But Jesus' disciples had actually witnessed the Son of God — the King of kings and Lord of lords — ascending to heaven to sit at his Father's right hand. They could travel the world and testify with confidence that Jesus, indeed, was the living Son of God.

Opening Thoughts (3 minutes)

The Very Words of God

> You will receive power when the Holy Spirit comes on you; and you will be my witnesses in Jerusalem, and in all Judea and Samaria, and to the ends of the earth.

Acts 1:8

Think About It

The Roman Empire was not an easy place in which to share the message of the kingdom of God. People were free to practice religions of their choice — as long as they honored Rome above all else. If one's religious practices threatened Rome's supremacy or security in any perceived way, however, the consequences could be severe.

Take a minute to think about the opportunities and risks of sharing the message of God's kingdom in your world. Which places, situations, attitudes, and beliefs make it difficult or risky to live out or share your faith?

DVD Teaching Notes (31 minutes)

Galilee—Jesus the rabbi builds a community of disciples

Caesarea Philippi—Jesus asks the all-important question

The Mount of Olives—Jesus delivers an unforgettable message

DVD Discussion (5 minutes)

1. Look carefully at the regions of Israel and Asia Minor on the map of the Roman Empire. What do you notice about the geographic and topographic characteristics of Asia Minor that would have made it a challenging place for Jewish disciples from Galilee to share the good news about Jesus? Consider, for example, the distances and means of travel. Notice

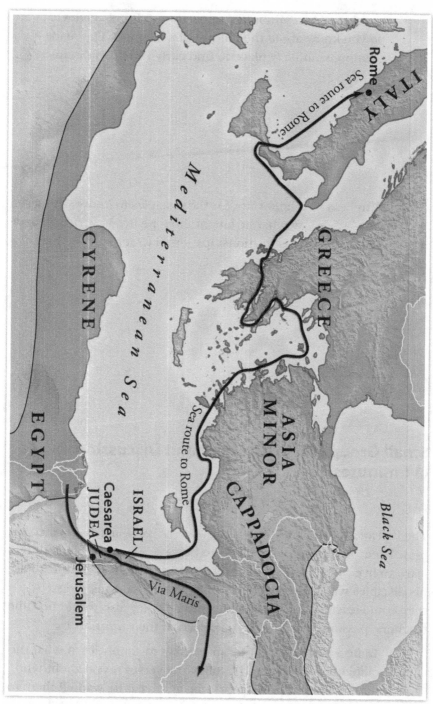

THE ROMAN EMPIRE

the size of Asia Minor in comparison to Israel. And what
do you know about the culture of Asia Minor that made it a
seemingly unlikely place to find early Christian disciples?

2. Why was it so important for the disciples to know who Jesus
    was — to know what he taught, how he lived every day, how
    he conducted his relationships — and to actually see him
    ascend to heaven?

Small Group Bible Discovery and Discussion (11 minutes)

Following the Example of the Rabbi

The disciples of a rabbi — *talmidim* — were passionately devoted to
him. Their overriding passion was to become like the rabbi and to
learn to live as he lived. As the rabbi lived and interpreted the Torah,
his disciples watched and noted everything he said and did so that
they could learn to do the same. Eventually, they also would become
teachers, passing on what they'd learned to their *talmidim*.

1. To be a *talmid* meant far more than to simply learn what the
    rabbi knew. What do the following verses reveal about who
    Jesus wanted his disciples to be and what he wanted them to
    do — how he wanted them to live out their faith daily?

Scripture Text	What It Meant to Be Like the Rabbi
Mark 3:13–15	
Luke 6:40	
Luke 9:1–6	
Luke 14:27	
John 8:31	
John 13:13–17	

2. In what ways is the picture of discipleship illustrated by these descriptions, teachings, and commands similar to or different from what we may understand discipleship to be?

3. What specific changes in our thinking and practice of discipleship might we need to make if we desire to make the kind of difference in our world that Jesus' disciples made in their world?

Faith Lesson (4 minutes)

On a mountaintop in Galilee, Jesus told his disciples, "All authority in heaven and on earth has been given to me. Therefore go and
make disciples of all nations, baptizing them in the name of the
Father and of the Son and of the Holy Spirit, and teaching them to
obey everything I have commanded you. And surely I am with you
always, to the very end of the age" (Matthew 28:18 – 20). Consider
not only the powerful and compelling message that these words
conveyed to Jesus' *talmidim* but what these words mean to you as
you live out your daily life and share his message in your world.

1. For what mission had Jesus trained his disciples, and why
   was teaching obedience so important in Israel and in the
   pagan provinces of the Roman Empire?

   Why is obedience to everything God commands important
   as you follow Jesus today?

2. How much authority did Jesus have, and how much would
   the disciples have? Why did they need to remember this?

   How does the authority of Jesus affect how you go about
   sharing his message in your world?

3. Why do you think it was important for Jesus' disciples to know that he would always be with them?

In what ways does this promise empower you to be a bold witness in your world?

Closing (1 minute)

Read Luke 24:45 – 49 aloud: "Then he opened their minds so they could understand the Scriptures. He told them, 'This is what is written: The Christ will suffer and rise from the dead on the third day, and repentance and forgiveness of sins will be preached in his name to all nations, beginning at Jerusalem. You are witnesses of these things. I am going to send you what my Father has promised; but stay in the city until you have been clothed with power from on high.' "

Jesus, our risen Savior, is in heaven and desires that each of us be an effective disciple. Pray together, asking him to give you the desire to be like him, to obey him in every way, and to proclaim his message of repentance and forgiveness to people in your family and neighborhood as well as in places that are foreign and frightening to you. Ask him to clothe you with his power and to make you effective witnesses of the living Christ.

Memorize

Then he opened their minds so they could understand the Scriptures. He told them, "This is what is written: The Christ will suffer and rise from the dead on the third day, and repentance and forgiveness of sins will be preached in his name to all nations, beginning at Jerusalem. You are witnesses of these things."

Luke 24:45 – 48

Conquering the Gates of Hell

In-Depth Personal Study Sessions

Day One | Jesus the Rabbi

The Very Words of God

> *Now there was a man of the Pharisees named Nicodemus, a member of the Jewish ruling council. He came to Jesus at night and said, "Rabbi, we know you are a teacher who has come from God. For no one could perform the miraculous signs you are doing if God were not with him."*

John 3:1 – 2

Bible Discovery

What Kind of Rabbi Was Jesus?

During Jesus' time, the term *rabbi* did not refer to a specific office or occupation. Rather, it was a term of respect, meaning "great one" or "my master." Day after day, a rabbi's *talmidim* would listen, watch, and imitate their rabbi in order to learn how to interpret the Scriptures and live in obedience to God. So Jesus' disciples accompanied him everywhere he went. They listened to his every word, watched what he did, and gained "hands-on" experience in seeing God work. The following passages of Scripture reveal a glimpse into how Jesus taught and interacted with his disciples.

1. A rabbi of Jesus' day encouraged his disciples to take on the "yoke of Torah," which meant to commit to obeying the Torah as the rabbi interpreted and taught it. How did Jesus describe his "yoke," and how did it compare to the "yoke" of some other rabbis? (See Matthew 11:28 – 30; 23:1 – 4.)

2. As the disciples observed Jesus teaching and interacting with people, how did they respond? (See Mark 10:17 - 28.)

3. What did Jesus do to ensure that his disciples "got it" — that they understood the meaning behind his parables? (See Mark 4:33 - 34.)

4. How did Jesus respond when his disciples requested teaching on prayer, and what does this say to you about what Jesus valued in his relationship with them? (See Luke 11:1 - 13.)

5. Jesus also taught his disciples through the circumstances of daily life. What lessons did Jesus teach his disciples through each of the following experiences?

   Matthew 14:22 - 33

   Mark 4:35 - 41

   Mark 5:1 - 13

Do you think the disciples ever forgot the lessons of these events? Why or why not?

DATA FILE
The Amazing Galileans

Jesus focused his ministry in one small place in Israel: Galilee, in the three cities of Korazin, Capernaum, and Bethsaida (Matthew 4:13–16; 11:20–24). Although many people today assume that Galileans were simple, uneducated peasants who lived in an isolated area, the truth is they interacted more with the world than the Jews of Jerusalem. After all, the Via Maris trade route passed through Galilee, exposing them to many different peoples and cultures.

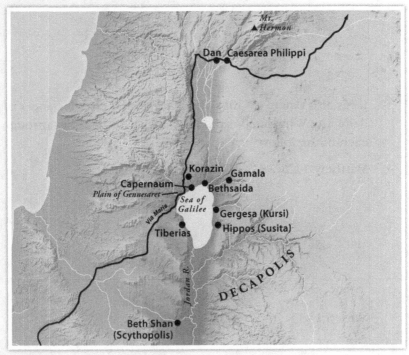

GALILEE OF JESUS' MINISTRY

Galileans were also the most religious Jews in the world during Jesus' time. They revered and knew the Scriptures well. They were passionately committed to living out their faith and passing their faith, knowledge, and lifestyle on to their children. This led to the establishment of vibrant religious communities; a strong commitment to families and country; and active participation in the local synagogues — the community centers of that day. In fact, more famous Jewish teachers came from Galilee than from any other part of Israel. Galileans also resisted the pagan influences of Hellenism far longer than their Judean counterparts. When the great revolt against the Romans and their collaborators finally occurred (AD 66 – 74), it began among Galileans.

Clearly God carefully prepared the environment in which Jesus was born and reared so that he would have exactly the context he needed in order to present his message of *malchut Shemayim* — the kingdom of heaven — effectively. The people of Galilee readily understood his message. Many of them joined his movement, and for at least the first fifty years after Jesus' ascension the Christian community remained strongest in Galilee.

A deeper knowledge of Galilee and its people helps us to understand the great faith and courage of his disciples who left Galilee and shared the good news throughout the world. (Evidence indicates that Judas Iscariot was apparently the only non-Galilean among Jesus' twelve, closest disciples.) The disciples' courage, the message they taught, the methods they used, and their complete devotion to God and his Word were born in Galilee's religious communities.

Reflection

How would you describe the relationship Jesus had with his disciples?

Why was Jesus' "yoke of Torah" different from that of other rabbis? What difference does this make as we seek to communicate Jesus and his truth with people in our culture?

What do you think making disciples — teaching people how to become like Jesus — looks like today? What challenges are involved in doing this?

Memorize

A student is not above his teacher, but everyone who is fully trained will be like his teacher.

Luke 6:40

Day Two | Teaching in Ways People Understand

The Very Words of God

You are the light of the world. A city on a hill cannot be hidden. Neither do people light a lamp and put it under a bowl. Instead they put it on its stand, and it gives light to everyone in the house. In the same way, let your light shine before men, that they may see your good deeds and praise your Father in heaven.

Matthew 5:14–16

Bible Discovery

Jesus Was a Powerful Communicator

When Jesus taught, he used word pictures and literal, concrete illustrations of familiar objects that made it easier for his listeners to understand his message. Later, as the disciples journeyed into Asia Minor to carry out his mandate, they used the same teaching method.

1. Which word picture did Jesus use when calling Simon Peter and Andrew to follow him, and why do you think this image would have been meaningful to them? (See Matthew 4:18 – 20.)

2. In Matthew 16:1 – 4, Jesus used the familiar images of sunrise and sunset to rebuke the Pharisees and Sadducees who had come to test him regarding miraculous signs from heaven. Do you think they understood what he was saying? Why or why not?

3. After the encounter of Matthew 16:1 – 4, Jesus used another common word picture as a metaphor to describe the Pharisees and Sadducees, but his disciples did not understand his meaning. (See Matthew 16:5 – 12.) What message(s) was Jesus conveying by using this image?

How did Jesus respond to his disciples' confusion, and what do you think they learned from this experience?

4. In Matthew 13:24 – 50, Jesus used a series of images to teach about the kingdom of heaven. As you read this text, take careful note of what each image teaches about the kingdom. Consider first what it would have communicated to the people of Jesus' day, then consider its significance to you.

The Kingdom of Heaven Is Like ...	What the Image Reveals about the Kingdom of Heaven
A man who sowed good seed, but ...	
A mustard seed ...	
Yeast mixed into dough ...	
A treasure hidden in a field ...	
A merchant looking for fine pearls ...	
A net let down into the lake ...	

5.   Why are these illustrations so memorable?

Reflection

Jesus ended his teaching about the kingdom of heaven by asking his disciples if they had understood everything he said. They said "yes," and Jesus responded to them with these remarkable words: "Therefore every teacher of the law who has been instructed about the kingdom of heaven is like the owner of a house who brings out of his storeroom new treasures as well as old" (Matthew 13:51 – 52)!

Which new and old treasures has Jesus given you to share?

What are the advantages (and possible disadvantages) of using word pictures to illustrate important truths as opposed to directly stating key points?

If you were to illustrate aspects of the Christian faith to someone who knows virtually nothing about Jesus and the Bible, how might you adapt this teaching style to communicate your message? Which word pictures might you use?

PROFILE OF A MASTER
Jesus the Master Teacher

The great teachers (rabbis) during Jesus' day used a technique that was later called *remez*. In their teaching, they would use part of a Scripture passage in a discussion, assuming that their audience's knowledge of the Bible would allow them to deduce for themselves the fuller meaning of the teaching. Jesus, who possessed a brilliant understanding of Scripture and strong teaching skills, used this method often.

For example, when the children shouted "Hosanna" to him in the temple and the chief priests and teachers of the law became indignant (Matthew 21:15), Jesus responded by quoting Psalm 8:2: "From the lips of children and infants you have ordained praise." The religious leaders' anger at Jesus can be better understood when we realize that the next phrase in the psalm reveals why children and infants offer praise—because the enemies of God would be silenced. The religious leaders realized that Jesus was implying that they were God's enemies.

Jesus used this teaching method again when speaking to Zacchaeus. "For the Son of Man came to seek and to save what was lost," Jesus said (Luke 19:10). The background to this statement is probably Ezekiel 34. God, angry with Israel's leaders for scattering and harming his flock, stated that he would become the shepherd and would seek the lost ones and save them. Based on this, the people of Jesus' day understood that the Messiah to come would "seek and save" the lost. By using this phrase, knowing that his listeners knew the Scripture, Jesus communicated several things. To the people, he communicated, "I am the Messiah and also God." To the religious leaders, whose influence kept Zacchaeus out of the crowd, he said, "You have scattered and harmed God's flock." To Zacchaeus, he said, "You are one of God's lost sheep, and he still loves you."

Jesus best fit the type of rabbi believed to have *s'mikhah,* the authority to make new interpretations of the Torah. Whereas most teachers of the law could only teach accepted interpretations, teachers with authority could make new interpretations and pass legal judgments. Crowds were amazed because Jesus taught with authority (Matthew 7:28–29), and some people questioned his authority (Matthew 21:23–27).

Day Three | Confronting the "Gates of Hades"

The Very Words of God

> *If anyone would come after me, he must deny himself and take up his cross and follow me.*
>
> **Mark 8:34**

Bible Discovery

Essential Lessons for Ministry in a Pagan World

Jesus took his disciples from their familiar Jewish religious surroundings in Galilee to the equally religious but incredibly pagan city of Caesarea Philippi about thirty miles away. Caesarea Philippi was a world center of Pan worship, the location of an annual Pan festival and an assortment of other pagan shrines. Here Jesus gave his disciples essential lessons that would prepare them for their future ministry in a pagan world.

1. Considering their location at Caesarea Philippi, why was Peter's use of the word "living" so significant when he

ARTIST'S RENDERING OF CAESAREA PHILIPPI

declared Jesus to be "the Christ, the Son of the living God"? (See Matthew 16:13 – 16.)

2. Matthew 16:17 – 18 is Jesus' first recorded referral to his "church," the new community he came to establish. It is also where Jesus mentioned the "rock" on which his church would be built, which has been the subject of much discussion throughout the history of Christianity.

    a. Given the setting in which this conversation took place — the "rock of the gods" at Caesarea Philippi where numerous statues of pagan gods were displayed in niches carved into the face of the cliff — what could be the symbolic meaning of Jesus' declaration, "on *this* rock I will build my church" [italics added]?

    b. The cave at the base of the cliff in Caesarea Philippi was called the "gates of Hades," and in this setting Jesus continued teaching about the building of his church. He boldly declared that "the gates of Hades will not overcome it." If the purpose of gates is to defend, who or what would be attacking the forces of Hades, and what did Jesus say will be the outcome of this conflict?

WORTH OBSERVING ...
The Meaning of the "Rock"

Throughout church history, there has been discussion and debate on exactly what Jesus meant when he said, "On this rock I will build my church" (Matthew 16:18). As explained in the video, the cliff face in Caesarea Philippi that was used for centuries in idol worship provides yet another metaphor for the "rock" Jesus mentioned. In this setting, the "rock" can mean the "rock" of pagan values and dead idolatry that was so prominent in Caesarea Philippi. Jesus, then, was saying that his church would replace those values.

Two other viewpoints within the traditional understanding of the meaning of the "rock" are:

- The "rock" is the confession of Peter that Jesus is the Christ (i.e., Christ, the Son of the living God, the foundation of the church. See Acts 4:10–11 and 1 Corinthians 3:10–15.)
- The "rock" is Peter, whose confession on behalf of the other disciples acknowledged the truth that Jesus is Messiah.

c. Would you say the church today generally views itself as being offensive or defensive in the battle against evil?

d. How might this view differ from what Jesus taught his disciples in Caesarea Philippi?

   e. How might an offensive vs. defensive mentality affect the way disciples minister in the world around them?

DID YOU KNOW?

"The gates of Hades," a phrase found in Matthew 16:18, can be translated as "hell." Hades, called *Sheol* in Hebrew, is where departed spirits live. Apparently it was frequently used as a synonym for hell. (See Psalm 9:17; 55:15; 116:3.)

3. Mark 8:34 – 9:1 broadens the picture of what Jesus taught in the vicinity of Caesarea Philippi.

   a. The text tells us that Jesus taught not only his disciples but the crowd as well. What types of people were probably present when Jesus addressed the crowd near Caesarea Philippi?

   b. When Jesus invited the crowd to "come after" him, what did he tell them they must do?

   c. In what ways would people who worshiped Pan and other gods have to "deny themselves" in order to follow Jesus? (See also 1 Peter 4:3 – 4 and 1 John 2:15 – 17.)

d. How might the disciples have felt when Jesus suddenly called out to the pagan crowd? What impact do you think his strong words about being ashamed of him had on his disciples that day and in the future when they went out into the pagan cultures of Asia Minor?

DATA FILE
Pagan Worship in Caesarea Philippi

At the foot of one of the ridges of Mount Hermon in northern Israel stands a one-hundred-foot cliff that for centuries held great significance to pagan worshipers. Here, an underground river (one of the fountainheads of the Jordan River) flowed from a large, deep cave called the Grotto of Pan. The cave was also known as the "gates of Hades" (hell) because pagan people believed that their gods used this cave to travel to and from the underworld.

As part of their fertility rituals, worshipers carved small niches into the cliff face to hold statues or idols of their gods. These included Pan and his sexual partners (nymphs) as well as other goddesses of fertility cults such as Nemesis from Phoenicia — the home of Asherah and Baal. Idols of Athena and Aphrodite have been unearthed at

THE GROTTO OF PAN

continued on next page . . .

this site, and Baal may have been worshiped here as well.

Several hundred years before Jesus visited this area with his disciples, Greek soldiers of Alexander the Great built a shrine dedicated to Pan—the fertility god of mountains and forests—on the flat area in front of the cliff face. A thirty-by-forty-five-foot platform served as the sacred place for Pan. Nearby, a Pan statue stood in a vaulted, artificial cave that contained niches holding the statues of nymphs who supposedly had sexual relations with Pan.

PAGAN GOD NICHE

In front of the cave, about 20 BC, Herod the Great built a small, thirty-by-sixty-foot temple of white marble dedicated to Emperor Augustus. During religious rites, animals were

THE TEMPLE PODIUM

sacrificed and thrown into the cave. If the water rushing out contained blood, the gods had rejected the sacrifice. This temple, which honored a human who called himself a god, greatly offended Jewish people (such as the disciples) who followed the Torah.

Near the cliff in which the cave was located, Herod the Great's son, Herod Phillip, built his capital city during Jesus' lifetime. He also enlarged the religious shrines. After Jesus' time, this location continued to be a focal point of pagan worship. A fifteen-by-forty-eight-foot Nemesis shrine, for example, was built to honor one of the nymphs of Pan—the goddess of revenge.

Emperor Trajan (AD 98–117) built a thirty-five-by-fifty-foot temple dedicated to Zeus in this same area. And, about AD 220, the forty-eight-by-sixty-foot Goat Shrine and the thirty-five-by-twenty-two-foot Court of the Dancing Goats were built. In both of these, worshipers feasted on sacrificed (possibly raw) meat, made sacrifices to Pan and other pagan deities, observed mating goats, and held religious celebrations. Sexual rituals (maybe even sexual relations between humans and goats) probably took place here as well. Nothing could have been more offensive to people who believed in God.

Reflection

The area immediately surrounding Caesarea Philippi was probably as spiritually removed from Galilee (and as much like Asia Minor) as any place in Israel. For that reason, it was the perfect place for Jesus to take his *talmidim* so they could see what he did and how he taught in the midst of a pagan culture. By being with Jesus in Caesarea Philippi, the disciples could begin to learn how to be like him in the world into which he would soon command them to go.

What do you think the disciples may have learned from their trip to Caesarea Philippi?

How might these truths relate to Christians today who face pagan cultures?

What did you learn about living as Jesus commands in the midst of a culture that chases after many different gods?

What desires did the pagan worshipers at Caesarea Philippi seek to fulfill through their rites?

How are these like the desires people seek to fulfill today?

In contrast, when we seek to fulfill the deep desires of life through a relationship with Jesus Christ, what ways of seeking meaning, purpose, and/or fulfillment must we abandon?

When Christians truly believe, as Peter declared he did, that Jesus is the Son of the living God, what difference does that make in how we live? In how we believe and think? In what we hope for? In what we do that we would otherwise not do?

How do you know you have the power to attack "the gates of hell" and overcome the pagan values of the world?

What specific things are you doing to challenge the forces of evil in your world?

When have you been ashamed of Jesus or his message and "back-pedaled" when someone has challenged your faith? What have been the consequences of your actions?

Which persons today do you respect and look up to because they boldly proclaim Jesus' message? How might following their example influence you to be bolder in proclaiming the gospel message, even if it might lead to persecution or hardship?

Memorize

Simon Peter answered, "You are the Christ, the Son of the living God."

Matthew 16:16

THINK ABOUT IT
A Legacy of Terrible Choices

Caesarea Philippi, where "the Gates of Hades" was located, developed as a pagan worship center in part because of the history of the city of Dan, only three miles away. Although God had given the tribe of Dan territory in the Shephelah between the coastal plain and the mountains of Judea, the Danites did not capture this land in the name of the Lord. Rather, they settled near the northern border of Israel in an area that was widely known for its pagan worship.

From the very beginning of their occupation of these lands, the Danites made terrible choices regarding their worship of pagan gods (Judges 18). After the death of King Solomon, when the nation of Israel split into two kingdoms — Israel in the north and Judah in the south — King Jeroboam sought to solidify his kingdom by setting up pagan shrines at Dan and Bethel (1 Kings 12:26 – 33). At these sites, he encouraged the people to worship golden calves, which he said had brought them out of Egypt. Thus Jeroboam began a tradition of persistent idol worship that eventually led to the destruction of Israel (2 Kings 17:16 – 23).

Perhaps when we face a choice between serving God or going with the flow of pagan culture, we will remember how long our sin can influence those who come after us and instead will choose to leave a legacy of obedience and service to God for future generations.

Day Four | The Power of *Talmidim*

The Very Words of God

> *We know that we have come to know him [Christ] if we obey his commands. The man who says, "I know him," but does not do what he commands is a liar, and the truth is not in him.... This is how we know we are in him: Whoever claims to live in him must walk as Jesus did.*

1 John 2:3 – 6

Bible Discovery

Prepared to Change the World

One reason the gospel message spread so rapidly during the days of the early church was because Jesus' disciples weren't simply people who heard his teachings and agreed with them. Rather, Jesus had called them to be his *talmidim:* chosen disciples who had a passion to not only know what Jesus knew, but to put his teachings into practice and to seek to live as he lived in every way. As Jesus' *talmidim*, the disciples in turn developed close relationships with others who also would become *talmidim*.

1. Jesus trained his *talmidim* by instruction and example, and also by giving them opportunities to practice what they were learning. On at least two occasions Jesus sent his disciples out into the world to minister to others. In each instance, note how Jesus instructed them, what the disciples did, and the result.

   a. Sending out the Twelve (See Luke 9:1 – 9.)

   b. Sending out the Seventy-two (See Luke 10:1 – 12; 17 – 20.)

    c. What impact would such personal experiences have had on your conviction and desire to be a totally committed, living witness of the message of Jesus?

2. As recorded in Matthew 28:16–20, Jesus gave his disciples their marching orders: to go into all the nations and teach others to be disciples who would obey everything Jesus had commanded. As you read each of the following passages, note the ways in which Jesus' disciples carried out his instructions.

    a. To whom was the message of Christ being taught? (See Acts 26:19–30.)

    b. In what ways were disciples training up new disciples? (See 1 Corinthians 4:15–17.)

    c. How important was it to model the message of Christ for others? (See 1 Thessalonians 1:6–7.)

d. What were believers to imitate? (See Hebrews 6:12; 13:7.)

WORTH OBSERVING ...
The Relationship That Changes the World

Jesus' disciples, the ones he called into relationship with him as *talmidim*, made such an impact on the province of Asia Minor—the most pagan of all the Roman provinces—that within a few decades it became the most Christian province in the Roman Empire. Jesus desires the same kind of relationship with his disciples today. To have that kind of relationship in our world means that we must:

- Know God's Word and Jesus' interpretation of it.
- Be passionate in our devotion to that Word and Jesus' example.
- Follow where Jesus leads us, even if we are not sure of the final destination.
- Live by his teaching, which means we must know that teaching well.
- Be obsessed with being like him as much as is humanly possible.
- Develop meaningful relationships with others so that they will observe us and seek to imitate our love, devotion to God, and our Jesus-like lifestyle. (See 1 Corinthians 2:16; 11:1; Galatians 3:26–27.)

By God's grace, people who have a totally committed relationship with Christ can change even the most pagan cultures—including our own.

Reflection

The disciples had the privilege of seeing firsthand who Jesus was, and the experience of being his *talmidim* changed them forever. By their faithful, passionate obedience to his teachings, the disciples went out into the world and showed Jesus to others. As they shared the mind, heart, and example of Christ, God used them to change their world — one disciple at a time. It is no different today. Disciples who change the world are those who have a totally committed relationship with Jesus and follow him with all their heart, mind, soul, and strength.

Would you call yourself a *talmid* — a disciple of Jesus who seeks to become like him in every way? Why or why not?

Review the characteristics of a true disciple in the "Worth Observing" box on page 43 and think about how you can live according to these characteristics in your world.

How passionate are you about becoming like Jesus? In which area(s) of your walk with Jesus do you need to focus more attention?

Which obstacles must you overcome or which sins must you turn away from in order to devote yourself fully to your relationship with Jesus?

What kind of a model of Christ are you? When people see you, do they see someone who is totally committed to following Jesus' teachings and seeks to be like him in every way?

Just as the seventy-two disciples experienced joy when they saw God's power at work, God also wants us to experience joy in serving him. When have you received at least a glimpse (and maybe much more) of God working through you, and how has that encouraged you to faithfully live according to Jesus' teachings?

Memorize

Whoever has my commands and obeys them, he is the one who loves me. He who loves me will be loved by my Father, and I too will love him and show myself to him.

John 14:21

THE TRUTH OF THE MATTER
The "Yoke" of the Kingdom of Heaven

Many Christians today recognize that salvation is a gift from God and place little emphasis on "keeping the law" of the Bible. While it is true that Jesus did away with "law keeping" by obeying the law completely and offering salvation through grace to everyone who trusts in him, it is also true that Jesus never suggested that obedience to the Word of God was any less important because of his completed work. In fact, he commanded his followers to "go and make disciples ... teaching them to *obey everything* I have commanded you" (Matthew 28:19–20, italics added).

If we are to be like Jesus—to be his disciples—we must desire to be like him in all ways, which includes obeying him as he obeys his Father. Just as obedience was vital to the first-century disciples who went to pagan regions and proclaimed God's way to live, obedience is vital to us today. If we are to impact our world for God, we must have the same commitment to the lifestyle God demands and Jesus exemplified.

Day Five | The Impact of Jesus' Ascension

The Very Words of God

After the Lord Jesus had spoken to them, he was taken up into heaven and he sat at the right hand of God. Then the disciples went out and preached everywhere, and the Lord worked with them and confirmed his word by the signs that accompanied it.

Mark 16:19 – 20

Bible Discovery

Understanding the Message of the Ascension

Forty days after Jesus rose from the dead, the disciples watched as he ascended to heaven from the Mount of Olives (Acts 1:9 - 12). This dramatic event provided a significant lesson in the disciples' preparation to carry the message of God's kingdom to the world. To Jews, the ascension was a powerful statement of Jesus' identity and proclaimed God's ultimate victory over the world, including the defeat of Rome and paganism. To the Gentile world, the ascension conveyed a radical message that would directly challenge the practice of emperor worship.

1. Centuries before Jesus came to earth as the Messiah, the prophet Daniel had a vision that would have been quite familiar to religious Jews of Jesus' day. Read Daniel 7:13 - 14, then read the following passages about Jesus' last teachings and his ascension to heaven. As you read, take note of the similarities between Daniel's vision and the ascension of Jesus. Then consider how what the disciples knew, what they saw, and what they heard would have affected them.

Ascension Text	Similarities to Daniel 7:13 – 14	Impact on the Disciples
Matthew 28:16 – 20		

Luke 24:50–53		
Acts 1:3–11		

2. How would news of what the disciples had witnessed first-hand have been received by the Roman world, especially the Roman authorities?

DID YOU KNOW?

When Jesus ascended to heaven, the movement to deify the Roman emperors was still in its early stages. After an emperor died, "witnesses" would come forth and claim to have seen the emperor ascend to heaven. Based on their testimony, the new emperor would then claim to be the son of a god. So when Jesus, the true Son of God, ascended to heaven, he was challenging the deity and authority of the Roman emperors! His radical message would lead to conflict throughout the Roman Empire. In Asia Minor, where emperor worship occurred the earliest and became the strongest, the message of Jesus' ascension led to the execution of most of his disciples.

Reflection

On the Mount of Olives, Jesus reminded his disciples that they were his witnesses to the world. Then, before their eyes, he ascended into heaven. This dramatic scene helped to inspire their faith and fuel their passionate commitment to boldly proclaim the message of Jesus to the world — no matter how great the cost.

What difference do you think Jesus' ascension ought to make in the lives of his disciples today? What real impact does it have on your faith and commitment?

The disciples knew that Jesus' coming to earth as the Messiah and his death, resurrection, and ascension fulfilled the ancient prophecies. Why is this important to recognize, and how might it help you communicate his message to people in your culture?

Jesus' ascension directly challenged the deity claims of the Roman emperors and those who worshiped them, so there was strong resistance to the message of the kingdom of God. Which beliefs and practices in our culture are challenged by the truth about Jesus, and what kind of resistance to the deity and authority of Jesus do Christians face today?

How do you respond to resistance, or even persecution, that comes as a result of the message of Jesus, and how deep is your commitment to obediently and faithfully proclaim it?

THE SALT OF THE EARTH

The ancient city of Sardis stood at the crossroads of Asia Minor, the most prosperous, powerful, fertile, and pagan province of the Roman Empire. The city was probably occupied first by Hittites, later by Lydians. Around 550 BC, Cyrus the Persian besieged the famous Lydian king, Croesus, who had fortified himself in the acropolis of Sardis atop Mount Tmolus. During the siege, a Persian soldier named Lagoras noticed that a Lydian soldier successfully retrieved a helmet that he had dropped from the top of the city wall. Concluding that there must be a secret trail into the city, Lagoras told Cyrus, and the Persian army crawled up that path at night and conquered the city. Centuries later, the Greeks captured the city because of a similar lapse in vigilance on the part of Sardinian defenders.

First-century Sardis had a unique blend of residents: faithful Jews and Christians who worshiped God as well as influential pagans who worshiped Artemis, Cybele, and the Roman emperor. Although a Christian presence in Sardis was highly visible, God, through the apostle John, issued a strong warning to its church: "I know your deeds; you have a reputation of being alive, but you are dead. Wake up! . . . But if you do not wake up, I will come like a thief, and you will not know at what time I will come to you" (Revelation 3:1 – 3). In light of their city's history, the Christians in Sardis probably had little doubt about the meaning of John's warning to stay watchful and alert in order to maintain their Christian walk.

Archaeological evidence suggests that Jews and Christians in Sardis openly displayed their faith. Jewish and Christian symbols — crosses, menorahs, rings with crosses in them, and even the "fish" symbol — have been discovered in many shops. A number of defaced pagan articles also have been found, including a lion-shaped lamp from which a pagan goddess had been removed. In one shop, Christian crosses had been chiseled over pagan symbols on tombstones that had been reused to make a dye vat.

One of the most impressive ruins in Sardis is that of the Greek gymnasium and Roman bathhouse. The gymnasium was the center of Greek culture, the means by which they passed on their Hellenistic worldview that the human being was the center of the universe. Within the gymnasium, students trained their bodies and minds. They studied literature, mathematics, philosophy, and medicine. They also enjoyed the pleasures and vices of the Roman baths.

Yet in one corner of that immoral, self-glorifying gymnasium, archaeologists have uncovered the largest synagogue of its time period! The presence of the synagogue within the gymnasium, as well as the presence of defaced pagan symbols within the synagogue — a table with Roman eagles, and pairs of lions that typically represented the goddess Cybele — beg the question "why?" Did the Jews of Sardis place their synagogue in the gymnasium in order to influence the culture, or had they so adopted the pagan lifestyle that they saw no discrepancy between worshiping God and participating in gymnasium activities?

A similar question arises regarding the most ancient ruins in Sardis, which originally was a shrine consecrated to Cybele. When the Greeks arrived about 330 BC, they absorbed the grossly immoral worship of Cybele into their worship of Artemis and built a huge temple — one of the seven largest Greek temples in the world — to Artemis, the Greek goddess of fertility. The ruins of this temple stand as a testimony to the popularity and power of the Artemis cult, but built into one corner of this great temple is a fourth-century Christian church. Why did Christians build a church there? Were they seeking to reclaim the temple for God, or had their worship of God blended in with pagan worship?

We don't know the answers to these questions, but they ought to cause us to consider our faithfulness to Jesus' command to be the "salt of the earth" (Matthew 5:13). As Christians, we are to build God's kingdom at the heart of our cultures, our communities, and our world. But we must be careful not to compromise our faith and lose our distinctiveness in the process.

Opening Thoughts (4 minutes)

The Very Words of God

> *You are the salt of the earth. But if the salt loses its saltiness, how can it be made salty again? It is no longer good for anything, except to be thrown out and trampled by men.*

> *Matthew 5:13*

Think About It

Salt doesn't do its job or fulfill its purpose until it is mixed in with what it is supposed to flavor. But salt that becomes diluted by what it is supposed to flavor can't do its job either.

If Christians are to be the salt of the earth, how involved with the secular world and secular people must we be in order to be "salt" and communicate the message of Jesus? How would you describe the difference between *involvement* that enables us to be salt and *compromise* that causes us to lose our saltiness?

DVD Teaching Notes (26 minutes)

John's warning

The history of Sardis

Standing for God in a pagan culture

    The shops

    The synagogue

    The church

Be the salt of the earth

DVD Discussion (6 minutes)

1. Which metaphor did John use to communicate God's message of warning to the church at Sardis?

What connection did the people of Sardis have with a "thief" who would come and take them by surprise?

What impact do you think John's choice of metaphor had on how his message was received?

**CHRISTIAN CHURCH (FOREGROUND)
IN THE TEMPLE OF ARTEMIS**

PROFILE OF A CITY
Sardis

- Stood in the middle of the Hermus River Valley, just over fifty miles east of the Mediterranean Sea in what is now the country of Turkey. The main east-west trade route came through this valley.
- On a spur of Mount Tmolus, above the Hermus River Valley, the Lydians—dominant people in the interior of Asia from about 1000–550 BC—built the acropolis of Sardis.
- As the capital of the Lydians, Sardis enjoyed half a millennium of artistic, architectural, and economic prosperity. Its most famous king, Croesus, became rich because his subjects discovered a way to "pan" gold from a nearby river using sheep fleeces that trapped flecks of gold.
- When Nebuchadnezzar conquered Assyria, Sardis became part of his empire. In 586 BC, he conquered Judah, destroyed Jerusalem and the temple, and exiled many Jews. Apparently many of them were brought to Sardis, and out of this community of Jews the church of Sardis was later born. It is amazing to see how God prepared things ahead of time to accomplish his purpose.
- The Persians made Sardis their western capital, so it remained an important city. Alexander the Great ended the Persian Empire in 334 BC, and Sardis became part of the Greek world.

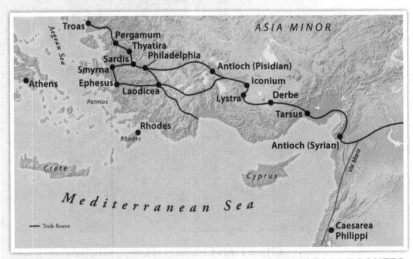

SARDIS TRADE ROUTES

2. Which of the archaeological discoveries presented in this video most surprised you and why?

What questions do these discoveries raise in your mind?

Small Group Bible Discovery and Discussion (13 minutes)

Witnesses without Compromise

On more than one occasion, Jesus told his disciples that they were to be "the salt of the earth" — to go into the world and live out the good news without compromise. He instructed them to retain their distinctiveness without isolating themselves from unbelievers. He cautioned them about the dangers of losing their "saltiness." Evidence in Sardis raises the question of whether the Jews and Christians who lived there influenced their pagan neighbors as God intended or whether they lost the distinctive beliefs and lifestyle that are essential to the life of faith and thereby compromised their calling. To better understand how Jesus wants his followers to live and fulfill God's calling in the world, let's further investigate the "salt" metaphor.

1. Where did Jesus want his disciples to demonstrate their faith, and how did he describe what he wanted them to be? (See Matthew 5:13; Mark 16:15.)

2. How would you describe what being "the salt of the earth" looked like in the world in which Jesus' disciples lived?

   In what ways would you say being salt in our world is like and unlike being salt in the predominately pagan world of the early disciples?

3. Jesus knew that being "the salt of the earth" would be a challenge. Note how he prayed for his disciples in John 17:6–9, 13–18.

   a. What did Jesus ask for on behalf of his disciples as they lived out their faith in a mostly pagan world? (See verse 15.)

   b. What is the significance of Jesus saying that his disciples were "not of the world any more than I am"?

   c. To what did Jesus compare the disciples' ministry, and why is this comparison so powerful? (See verse 18.)

d. In light of the way that Jesus prayed for his disciples, how important do you think it is for Christians today to take seriously Jesus' command to be salt in the world? Which of his words help you realize the importance of living as a witness without compromise?

DID YOU KNOW?

Salt was very valuable during Jesus' day. It aided in the preservation of meat and enhanced the taste of food. But another less commonly known use of salt helps us better understand what it means to be salt in our world.

Galileans used dome-shaped ovens made of hardened mud. Salt was mixed with dried dung, a common fuel, because the chemical reaction made the dung burn hotter and longer. Over time, however, salt lost the qualities that made it effective. So when it was no longer fit even for being mixed with manure, the "saltless" salt was thrown out.

As believers, we are not to be isolated from unbelievers. God calls us to go out into an evil world and "mix" with sinful people. Yet as we faithfully live out the good news in our world, we must keep our distinctive Christian identity. We must guard against absorbing the values of the pagan world and losing the qualities that make us "salt."

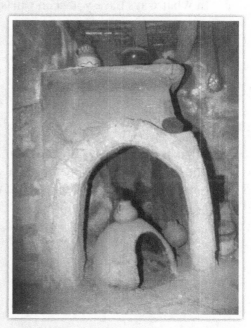

GALILEAN OVEN

Faith Lesson (5 minutes)

Jesus doesn't leave any doubt about the importance of his disciples being salt in the world. He says that when salt loses its saltiness it is not good for anything — not even the manure pile (Matthew 5:13; Luke 14:34 – 35).

1. What do you think are the biggest challenges facing a Christian who is committed to following Jesus and being salt?

2. In what ways have you seen Christians lose their saltiness?

3. What specific things do you do to guard against losing your saltiness — the distinctive beliefs and lifestyle that are essential to being a follower of Jesus — while also being involved in the world around you?

Closing (1 minute)

Read Luke 14:34 – 35 aloud: "Salt is good, but if it loses its saltiness, how can it be made salty again? It is fit neither for the soil nor for the manure pile; it is thrown out. He who has ears to hear, let him hear."

As Christians, our challenge is to retain our distinctiveness — our saltiness — as we interact with people who have not yet accepted Jesus as their Lord and Savior. Ask God to guide and strengthen you in being salt every day. Invite him to give you opportunities to share his message as you go about your life and to honor him in all that you think, say, and do.

Memorize

> *Salt is good, but if it loses its saltiness, how can it be made salty again? It is fit neither for the soil nor for the manure pile; it is thrown out. He who has ears to hear, let him hear.*
>
> **Luke 14:34 – 35**

Conquering the Gates of Hell

In-Depth Personal Study Sessions

Day One | God Has a Strategy for His Witnesses

The Very Words of God

> *You will receive power when the Holy Spirit comes on you; and you will be my witnesses in Jerusalem, and in all Judea and Samaria, and to the ends of the earth.*

Acts 1:8

Bible Discovery

God's Strategy Unfolds

God has always intended for his people to live in the midst of culture and to live in such a way that the world would come to know who he is. The people of Israel were his witnesses as they possessed the Promised Land. The disciples and early Christians were his witnesses as they went out and began to share the good news of Jesus in the cities and synagogues of Asia Minor.

1. What was the mission of the Old Testament followers of God? (See 1 Samuel 17:45 - 47; Isaiah 43:10 - 12.)

2. What was the mission of the early Christian missionaries? (See Acts 1:8; 10:37 - 43.)

DID YOU KNOW?
God Prepared Sardis to Receive the Good News

Jesus commanded his followers to "go into all the world and preach the good news to all creation" (Mark 16:15; Acts 1:8). It took his followers a while to understand the good news and what "*all* the world" [italics added] meant, but as the Holy Spirit opened their hearts and minds, they began to go. Was the world prepared for them and their life-changing message? The answer is a resounding "yes!"

God had a specific strategy in mind for sharing his message of salvation with the world. In Romans 1:16, Paul summarized it this way: "I am not ashamed of the gospel, because it is the power of God for the salvation of everyone who believes: *first* for the Jew, then for the Gentile [italics added]."

God commanded his people to reach the Jews first. Why? The Jews were expecting the Messiah and already were prepared to understand the gospel message. The Jews knew their Scriptures and would readily see how Jesus fulfilled the ancient prophecies. Also, God may have wanted Jews in each community to help Gentiles understand the roots of their newfound faith. So when Paul, Silas, Barnabas, and other believers traveled to new locations, they went to the local synagogues and preached the news of Jesus Christ there. (See Acts 9:20; 13:5, 14; 14:1; 17:1 – 2, 10 – 12; 18:1 – 7, 19; 19:8.)

Although we don't know who started the church in Sardis, Jews were already living there when early Christian missionaries arrived with the gospel. In fact, hundreds of years before Jesus came to earth, God used pagan rulers to scatter Jewish populations across Asia Minor. It is likely that Nebuchadnezzar of Babylon exiled Jews to Sardis (2 Kings 25) when he destroyed Jerusalem in 586 BC. Later, Cyrus of Persia encouraged more Jews to move to Asia Minor, and Antiochus — the pagan Greek king — brought two thousand Jewish families to Asia Minor during the third century BC.

Some descendants of these exiled Jews were in Jerusalem during Pentecost (Acts 2:9); others lived in cities such as Sardis — a key, influential city at the crossroads of the world. The Jewish presence in Asia Minor dramatically increased the impact and spread of the gospel. Truly God is in control of all

continued on next page . . .

things. All things work toward his plan (Romans 8:28), and God can use evil for good (Genesis 50:20).

Today, God still has a plan and does "advance" preparation. Often the hearts of unbelievers are already open to receiving the message of the Messiah. So it is important for us to be faithful to God's call and depend on him to bring the spiritual fruit.

3.   Wherever he went — in homes, on mountainsides, along the roadside, in towns and villages — Jesus often taught crowds of people who came to see him. In which other locations did Jesus teach, and what might have been his purpose in teaching there? (Read Matthew 13:54; Mark 14:49.)

4.   Read the following accounts of the work of early Christian missionaries and take note of where they testified about Jesus. In light of Romans 1:16, consider why they taught in these locations and how this strategy helped accomplish God's purpose.

Scripture Text	The Message of Jesus Goes Out into the World
Acts 9:17–21	
Acts 13:1–5	
Acts 13:13–16	

Acts 14:1	
Acts 17:1–4	

Reflection

Long before Jesus' disciples received their commission to "go and make disciples of all nations" (Matthew 28:19), God was already preparing people in Asia Minor to receive his message. When the early Christian missionaries began living and teaching that message in Asia Minor, many people received it eagerly. As Christians today, we are God's witnesses to the people of our world. People are ready and waiting to see who God is, and God's strategy is for us to live in such a way that they will see us and know that he is God.

What are the strategic spheres of influence in which you live every day? (Home? Office? Community leadership? Family?)

Which ways of living and sharing the message of Jesus have you found to be most effective in reaching people in these areas?

In what ways have you failed to live out Jesus' message in these areas?

What is your commitment to live out Jesus' message in these areas, and what do you need to do differently in order to fulfill your mission?

Among other places, Jesus taught in the temple courts and synagogues where people who would readily understand his message gathered. What do you see as the "temple courts" and "synagogues" in which God calls you to be his witness today?

In what ways are you sharing the message of Jesus effectively in these places, and in what ways do you need to improve?

As you consider how God prepares people to receive his message, how does it affect your commitment to broaden the scope of your witness? Into which areas might God want you to expand your witness?

Memorize

"You are my witnesses," declares the L*ORD*, *"and my servant whom I have chosen, so that you may know and believe me and understand that I am he. Before me no god was formed, nor will there be one after me. I, even I, am the* L*ORD*, *and apart from me there is no savior.... You are my witnesses," declares the* L*ORD*, *"that I am God."*

Isaiah 43:10 – 12

Day Two | Sent Out to Challenge a Human-Centered Worldview

The Very Words of God

> *All the ends of the earth will remember and turn to the LORD, and all the families of the nations will bow down before him, for dominion belongs to the LORD.*

> **Psalm 22:27 – 28**

Bible Discovery

Understanding the Worldview Conflict

As the early Christian missionaries spread Jesus' message, they encountered views of the world and the nature of truth that differed greatly from their own. The conflict between a God-centered world-view and a human-centered worldview remains to this day — just as it has since the garden of Eden. Will people acknowledge God as the supreme being in the universe, or will they insist on claiming to be their own authority? Do human beings determine truth, or is God the source of all truth?

1. According to the worldview presented in the Bible, who is the ultimate, sovereign authority in the universe? (See Psalm 22:27 – 29; Isaiah 29:13 – 16; Romans 9:20 – 21.)

2. Genesis 3:1 – 7 reveals how Satan tempted Eve in the garden of Eden.

    a. In which ways did Satan's tempting offer to Eve challenge a God-centered worldview?

b. Which alternative worldview(s) did Satan offer?

c. In which ways is this conflict played out in our world, and in your life, today?

A STUDY IN CONTRASTS

Hellenism, the dominant worldview during the first century, stands in stark contrast to the truths of God found in the Bible.

Underlying Assumptions of a Hellenistic Worldview	Underlying Assumptions of a God-Centered Worldview
Gods are given the image of men and women.	Only God is God. He is the Lord of the universe who has created men and women in his image.
The human mind is the greatest source of wisdom.	God is the ultimate source of all wisdom.
Human beings determine truth—what is right and wrong.	God, the source of truth, has given us the standards that determine what is right and wrong.
Human accomplishment is the goal of life.	The goal of life is to glorify and serve God and thereby serve other people.
The human spirit finds fulfillment as we enjoy the rewards of leisure and pleasure.	The human spirit finds fulfillment as we honor God by serving others and making meaningful contributions to our world.
The human body and what human beings create is the highest standard of beauty.	Human beings create beauty because they are made in the image of God.

3. In what ways does Paul's message in 1 Corinthians 1:18 – 30 challenge a Hellenistic worldview? List as many as you can find! Then, consider how his message challenges the worldview of the culture in which you live.

4. Paul was so effective in challenging the Hellenistic worldview in Athens that he was asked to address the Areopagus, the equivalent of the city council. As you read this account in Acts 17:16 – 34, notice how respectfully yet thoroughly he refuted the assumptions of a Hellenistic worldview. What do you learn from this that can help you present a God-centered worldview in your world?

5. First John 2:15 – 16 makes it clear that we cannot live with both a worldview that recognizes God as the ultimate being and rightful authority for life and a "world" or human-centered view; we must choose one or the other. The following passages provide a mere sampling of Scripture's many warnings against adopting anything other than a God-centered worldview.

   a. What happens when people consider something or someone other than God to be the ultimate authority? (See Romans 1:18 – 32.)

b. Since the beginning of humanity, Satan has attacked God's supremacy by seeking to eliminate the God-centered worldview and replacing it with his own. What do you learn about the significance and consequences of this conflict from Jude 3 – 8?

DATA FILE
The Greek Gymnasium

Every major Hellenistic city had an educational institution called a gymnasium in which citizens of the Greek/Roman community were taught the wisdom of Hellenism. Religious Jews during biblical times believed the gymnasium to be an abomination because (1) education there was based on the view that humans are the ultimate source of truth, (2) many activities took place in the nude, and (3) students had to make certain pagan religious commitments in order to participate.

GYMNASIUM OF SARDIS

Several passages in Paul's writings imply that he was aware of gymnasiums: 1 Timothy 4:8 includes the expression "physical training" that is based on the Greek word for *gymnasium*; 1 Corinthians 9:24 – 27 mentions competitions such as boxing and running; and Galatians 2:2; 5:7 and Philippians 2:16 mention running. In Galatians 3:24, Paul also used the Greek word *paidago-*

gos, which referred to the slave attendant who accompanied students from wealthy families to school in order to tutor them in the lessons they received in the gymnasium.

Features of the Gymnasium at Sardis

The Palaestra

In this large (six hundred by one hundred fifty feet) open area to the east of the Marble Court, physical education took place on the sand floor. Smaller rooms around the outside were also used for physical training — conditioning (weights and calisthenics), skill development (discus, javelin, jumping), and cardiovascular training (running). In these rooms students also relaxed with massage and oil treatments after their exercise and classroom learning.

The Didaskelion

Students learned and recited lessons in rooms for academics located on the outside of the open area. There were three levels of education: elementary (boys and girls ages five to twelve who studied reading and writing); secondary (boys and girls ages twelve through sixteen who studied philosophy, math, science, and music); and advanced (boys ages sixteen through adulthood who studied philosophy, medicine, music, and science).

The Marble Court

This three-story, colonnaded courtyard was dedicated to the cult of the Roman emperor — believed to be the guardian of the truth being taught and exemplified in his life. All learning was devoted to him. Many niches in the walls served as pediments for statues. In the main apse was a statue of the emperor, who was honored with sacrifices and ceremonies during the educational process.

The Bath Complex

In the western section was the largest pool, the heated caldarium. East of this was a large, central hall and the warm pool (tepidarium). A nearby oblong hall held the cold pool (frigidarium) where students completed their bathing. There were also fountains in niches in the walls.

continued on next page . . .

The Synagogue

Holding more than one thousand people (estimated), this is the largest synagogue ever found in the ancient world. It was not part of the original gymnasium but was added later, just after the time of the New Testament. Here impressive mosaic floors added to the beauty of the structure and testify to the community's wealth. More than eighty inscriptions have been found in the

SYNAGOGUE IN THE GYMNASIUM

synagogue that indicate that some Jews had significant status and wealth in Sardis and that others in the congregation were Gentile converts.

Reflection

The early Christian missionaries understood the conflict between God-centered and human-centered worldviews, and they relentlessly challenged the authority of the Hellenistic value system. How do we follow their example and fight this battle? Peter summed it up in a letter to his friends: "I urge you, as aliens and strangers in the world, to abstain from sinful desires, which war against your soul. Live such good lives among the pagans that ... They may see your good deeds and glorify God" (1 Peter 2:11 – 12).

> What are some of the sinful desires that war against your soul, and in what ways do these thoughts and actions reflect an underlying Hellenistic or human-centered worldview?

In what subtle (or not-so-subtle) ways do you act as if you can create your own truth and make up your own rules rather than obeying God's truth?

How have these thoughts and actions affected your walk with God?

How have they affected your witness to a watching world?

What is your commitment to recognize God as Lord of the universe and the supreme authority in your life? What will you do to keep him at the center of your life?

In terms of representing and advocating a particular worldview, how do you think the education system of the ancient gymnasium compares with our public education system today?

Which other arenas of culture establish and promote a particular worldview?

How aware are you of what is being taught about a human-centered worldview through these arenas of culture?

How might you personally respond to and influence these arenas for Christ?

DID YOU KNOW?

First-century synagogues were more than just places of worship. They served as community centers for Jewish life. In the synagogue, the Jews prayed, taught school, held legal court, celebrated special events, and even lodged travelers. This may help us to understand why the synagogue in Sardis was located in the pagan gymnasium. The center of Jewish teaching was placed within the center of Hellenistic teaching.

SYNAGOGUE IN SARDIS

Day Three | Standing for God in a Pagan World

The Very Words of God

> *If you belonged to the world, it would love you as its own. As it is, you do not belong to the world, but I have chosen you out of the world. That is why the world hates you.*
>
> John 15:19

Bible Discovery

Finding the Balance between Being "in" the World but Not "of" the World

Everyone who is a follower of Christ is called to stand for God in the midst of culture, but it is not easy to do. Being involved enough in the culture to display our faith also puts us at risk for compromising with the values of the culture we are supposed to influence! We can, however, learn some things that will help us display our faith without succumbing to the beliefs or values of our everyday world.

1. God has often placed his people in the midst of evil cultures and called upon them to reflect his righteousness in those cultures.

   a. What terminology did God use to describe Israel's neighbors who worshiped pagan gods, and what words of caution did he give his people? (See Exodus 34:15 – 16.)

   b. How did Paul describe the worshipers of pagan gods in his day, which would include his "neighbors" in Asia Minor? (See Romans 1:22 – 25.)

   c. How do you think God would describe the beliefs and
      values of "neighbors" in your culture?

2. Where does a Christian's true citizenship lie, and how does
   this affect our role in our culture? (See Philippians 3:20;
   2 Corinthians 5:20.)

3. What did Jesus recognize as the great risk of being his
   ambassador, and what did he pray for his followers as they
   fulfilled their role in the world? (See John 17:15 – 16.)

4. What was Paul's commitment to proclaim and live out his
   faith, and how did he go about doing it? (See 1 Corinthians
   9:19 – 23.)

   What freedom did Paul claim in order to live out his faith?

5. Although Paul was willing to "become all things to all men ... for the sake of the gospel" (1 Corinthians 9:22 – 23), he also specified certain kinds of people with whom a believer must not associate. (See 1 Corinthians 5:9 – 11.)

   a. Under which specific conditions should a believer separate from people who practice such behaviors, and to which people did Paul say this prohibition does not apply?

   b. How do the distinctions Paul makes help you understand what it means to be "in" the world but not "of" the world?

Reflection

If you are a believer, you are an "ambassador" for Christ, and God is making his appeal to the world through you.

On a scale of one (poor) to ten (well), how are you doing as an ambassador for Christ?

In which areas do you find it most difficult to stand for God in daily life?

In which areas have you backed away from your mission and refused to be "in" the world? Why, and what are you willing to do differently?

In which areas have you crossed the line between being "in" the world and "of" the world? Why, and what are you willing to do differently?

In what ways do your relationships with other believers help or hinder you in being "in" the world but not "of" the world?

What is at risk when you associate with Christians who are rebellious against God and his Word?

Memorize

You adulterous people, don't you know that friendship with the world is hatred toward God? Anyone who chooses to be a friend of the world becomes an enemy of God.

James 4:4

Day Four | Live Up to Your Reputation!

The Very Words of God

> *I know your deeds; you have a reputation of being alive, but you are dead. Wake up! Strengthen what remains and is about to die, for I have not found your deeds complete in the sight of my God. Remember, therefore, what you have received and heard; obey it, and repent.*

> *Revelation 3:1–3*

Bible Discovery

John's Warning to the Church in Sardis

The history of Sardis and the archaeological discoveries made there provide valuable insights into the meaning and significance of the apostle John's warning to the church in that ancient city. His warning also applies to us and our faith communities as we face the challenge of living for God in our world. Read Revelation 3:1–6, then answer the following questions in light of the historical and/or archaeological evidence presented in the video and study sessions.

1. What paradox existed concerning the church in Sardis, and in what ways may the church that was later built in the Artemis temple reflect this? (See verse 1.)

2. What did John tell the Christians of Sardis to do? (See verse 2.)

3. Which specific steps toward reconciliation with God did John mention? (See verse 3.)

4. Which consequences did John say would be forthcoming if
    they did not change their ways? (See verse 3.)

5. What do we learn about some of the Christians in Sardis, and
    what hope did John promise to them and others like them?
    (See verses 4 – 5.)

WORTH OBSERVING ...
An Unlearned Lesson

About 550 BC, the Persians captured the Acropolis of Sardis after a Persian
soldier named Lagoras saw a soldier from Sardis climb down a steep, hidden trail to retrieve his helmet. Amazingly, a similar situation occurred again
about 200 BC! A Greek soldier named Hyroeades watched a soldier of Sardis
throw garbage off the top and noticed that vultures would wait on the wall
until the garbage was discarded again. So, the Greeks realized that a portion
of the wall was unguarded and captured the city by attacking that spot at
night.

Reflection

The rulers and defenders of Sardis paid a high price for not being
vigilant about the protection of their city. In both 550 BC and 200 BC,
Sardis fell to surprise attacks when the city was at the height of its
power. John warned the church in Sardis that they, too, would pay a
high price for their lack of vigilance if they did not change their ways.
Perhaps, like their ancient city, the church in Sardis had never been
better — never stronger, never more faithful. Perhaps John was warning them against being so confident of their "success" that they would
overlook the danger signs of weakness that could lead to their demise.
John's message to the church in Sardis is a warning to us as well.

What will happen to your witness before a watching world if you are not careful to stay alert to what is going on in your Christian walk?

In what way(s) — even small ways — have you been careless or apathetic about living out your faith?

Which particular sin(s) do you need to repent of in order to straighten out your relationship with God? Be specific.

What have you learned about what is required to walk faithfully with God from a time in your life, or in the life of a church community, when a surprising moment of weakness was exposed during a period of great faith and strength?

Which specific changes do you need to make or steps do you need to take in order to strengthen your walk with God and put new life into your witness in the world?

Memorize

Because of his great love for us, God, who is rich in mercy, made us alive with Christ.

Ephesians 2:4 – 5

Day Five | Living for God in Your World

The Very Words of God

You are a chosen people, a royal priesthood, a holy nation, a people belonging to God, that you may declare the praises of him who called you out of darkness into his wonderful light.

1 Peter 2:9

Bible Discovery

Will You Be Salt in Your World?

Today, just as during the days of the early church, God calls Christians to be witnesses of Jesus Christ through our words and deeds. Ours is not an easy task, but the words of Peter are a powerful reminder of who we are, what God has done for us, and how we can live in such a way that others will come to know God. Read 1 Peter 2:9 – 12, then answer the following questions.

1. In what ways do Peter's words present a worldview that is in opposition to a Hellenistic (human-centered) worldview? Write down specific examples.

2. What makes Christians "aliens and strangers in the world," and how does this terminology help us focus on living out our faith in everyday life?

3. What role does the obedience of God's people play in how the world recognizes and responds to him?

Reflection

Take some time to consider how deep your commitment to be salt in your world is.

In which ways are you being salt in the world, and in which ways may you be avoiding the world and thereby missing opportunities to share Jesus' message? Write down specific examples of both. (Be honest!)

I am salt in the world:	I am avoiding the world:

As you consider the world in which you live, what things do people who do not know God notice in another person's life that would cause them to glorify God?

How, without saying a word, might you share with people around you that you believe in Jesus?

Reread 1 Peter 2:9 – 12, imagining that he wrote it just for you. Let his words be an encouragement to engage with your culture without compromise and to fulfill God's calling to make him known to all the world.

WHERE SATAN LIVES

The apostle John introduced his letter to Christians who lived in Pergamum (Revelation 2:12 – 17) as being "the words of him who has the sharp, double-edged sword." This introduction is significant because Pergamum was the provincial capital of Asia Minor, and the Roman governor in that city had what was known as "the right of the sword" — Rome's authority to decide which prisoners or accused persons would live or die (including Christians who refused to honor Caesar as god). So John's letter begins with a bold assertion that would have been especially meaningful to the Christians of Pergamum: Jesus, not the Roman governor, ultimately has power over life and death.

John also gave Pergamum an unusual designation: "I know where you live — where Satan has his throne. Yet you remain true to my name. You did not renounce your faith in me, even in the days of Antipas, my faithful witness, who was put to death in your city — where Satan lives" (Revelation 2:13). The place where Satan lives, or has his throne, can mean any place that has no room for God — any place where God is not given the credit he deserves. In Pergamum there were many candidates for this designation. Some include:

- **The beautiful temple of Dionysus that stood prominently on the Acropolis.** Believed to be the offspring of a human mother and Zeus, the king of the gods, Dionysus was worshiped as the son of a god. He was believed to turn water into wine, and his followers hoped to gain life after death through their indulgence in raw meat and wine. By drinking wine to excess, his followers became "one" with him.

- **The temple shrine of Asclepius—the snake god of healing.** People who needed healing (but not the terminally ill or pregnant women who were ready to deliver) went to the elaborate hospital complex of Asclepius. There, patients were led through an underground tunnel to a huge treatment room where they went to sleep and waited to receive a vision of treatment from Asclepius. Once healed, patients bowed down on their knees before a statue of Asclepius, thanked him for their healing, gave him gifts, and—as a testimony to the god—inscribed on large, white stones their names and the ailments from which they had been cured.

- **The shrine of Demeter, the goddess of grain, who was most popular among middle- and lower-class women.** Demeter was a gentle goddess who supposedly provided food. Although most of the rituals of the Demeter cult were secret, her followers were known to immerse or wash themselves in the blood of a bull to receive cleansing for their sins.

- **The gigantic altar to Zeus, or perhaps the Athena temple where, beginning with Caesar Augustus, the Roman emperor was worshiped as both god and king.** As one of the disciples who had stood on the Mount of Olives and watched Jesus ascend to heaven, John knew beyond a doubt that Jesus, not Caesar Augustus or any other emperor, was seated at the right hand of God.

Satan wanted people to think that everything they needed for life—even eternal life—could be found through their own efforts or through the world around them. But God strategically placed the early believers in an evil world to stand as witnesses to his power and work in their lives. To those faithful witnesses, John offered his closing words: "I will also give him a white stone with a new name written on it, known only to him who receives it" (Revelation 2:17). The world needed to see that these believers, as standing stones for God, were clearly different from the white stones on which people "healed" by Asclepius had written their names.

Opening Thoughts (4 minutes)

The Very Words of God

> *Although they knew God, they neither glorified him as God nor gave thanks to him, but their thinking became futile and their foolish hearts were darkened. Although they claimed to be wise, they became fools and exchanged the glory of the immortal God for images made to look like mortal man and birds and animals and reptiles.*
>
> *Romans 1:21 – 23*

Think About It

All of us long for the satisfaction of finding a sense of meaning and significance in life, but we seek it in different ways.

What are some of the ways people today try to find meaning and significance in life apart from God? How do these people respond, and what kinds of cultural pressure do they exert, when they encounter people who find meaning and significance by living in submission to God's authority?

DVD Teaching Notes (25 minutes)

The city of Pergamum — where Satan has his throne

Temples to counterfeit gods
    Dionysus

    Asclepius

    Demeter

Others

The true source of meaning in life

PROFILE OF A CITY
Pergamum

Pergamum (now Bergama in Turkey) was located in the northern part of the Roman province of Asia Minor, along the Caicus River about ten miles from the Aegean Sea. From the third century BC until well into the fourth century AD, its kings controlled a major trade road from the east (Persia) to the Mediterranean world.

Following the city's conquest by Alexander the Great in 334 BC, its strategic location was recognized by Lysimachos, who turned it into a military base. From that point on, it became an increasingly significant Hellenistic

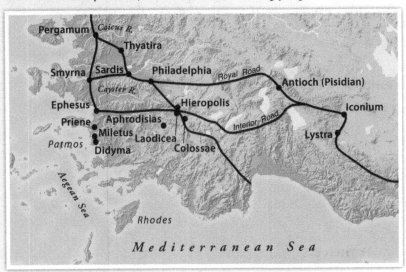

TRADE ROUTES OF ASIA MINOR

PERGAMUM

city—rich in culture, spectacular in architecture, and influential in its worship of pagan gods.

King Attalos III, the last king of Pergamum, willed the city to the Roman Empire so that its glory would not be spoiled by war. This proved to be a wise move because the Romans, who respected its cultural glory and religious character, made Pergamum the capital of the province of Asia Minor for a period of time. The Romans also left their mark when Pergamum became the first city in which worship of the Caesars as divine beings was established.

DVD Discussion (6 minutes)

1. What surprised you about the variety of ways in which Satan counterfeited the claims of Jesus in Pergamum?

2. What parallels do you see between the worship of the various gods of Pergamum and the priorities of our own culture?

3. How would you define what John meant by "Satan's throne" and the place "where Satan lives"?

In what ways could the everyday beliefs and activities of our culture be identified as the place "where Satan lives"?

Small Group Bible Discovery and Discussion (14 minutes)

Desperate for the "Good Life"

The worship of pagan gods in Pergamum encouraged people to seek what they needed in life from a source other than God, whether that need was the promise of physical healing, the provision of food, the forgiveness of sins, or immortality. But the life Satan offered through the worship of pagan gods was merely a deceptive imitation of the life God graciously gives to those who honor and obey him.

1. Even though Satan is clever and deceptive in luring people away from God, what excuse do people have for rejecting God's truth and why? (See Romans 1:18 – 25.)

2. What are the consequences of rejecting God's truth and pursuing life apart from him? (See Romans 1:21 – 26, 28.)

    Which examples of these consequences were evident in Pergamum, "where Satan lives"?

    In what ways does indulgence in what Paul calls "sinful desires" appear to provide the "good life"?

3. It's easy to make excuses for sinful behavior that is accepted as "normal" in culture. But Galatians 5:19 – 25 draws a clear contrast between the acts of the sinful nature and the acts of a person who lives by the Spirit.

    a. How obvious would the acts of the sinful nature mentioned here be to a person who lives by the Spirit? Why?

    b. In contrast, how obvious might they be to a person who does not live by the Spirit?

    c. What is the difference in testimony between a Christian who gives in to acts of the sinful nature versus one who lives by the Spirit, and what kind of an impact would each have on a watching world?

Faith Lesson (5 minutes)

Satan wants people to believe that meaning and significance — even eternal life — can be found through themselves, false gods, or the world around them. He still offers this temptation to us today.

1. In what way(s) — obvious and subtle — are you tempted to try to find "life" apart from God?

2. Which gods of this world appeal most to you, and in what ways do you make excuses to indulge in your sinful nature and follow them rather than keeping in step with the Spirit?

3. In which specific area(s) do you need to "crucify" your sinful nature, reaffirm your submission to Christ's lordship, and take steps to live more in step with his Spirit?

THE TRUTH OF THE MATTER
Giving God the Honor He Is Due

Satan has always wanted to rob God of the credit and honor due him. Because the deified emperors and gods of Pergamum such as Asclepius, Demeter, Dionysus, and Zeus received credit and honor that was due God alone, they were demonic counterfeits. Things haven't changed much in our world today. Satan still wants us to believe that we have the authority to decide what's ours, what's right and wrong, and so on.

Our culture has bought into Satan's lie. People today (most Christians included) act as if credit is due the hard worker, educated and successful people, people who care for their physical bodies properly, etc. But this perspective denies that God alone is Lord and provides everything we need—food, health, joy, wealth, etc. As the pagan cults of Pergamum illustrate, there is no place for God when we assume that perspective. *Anyone who fails to give God the credit he deserves is where Satan lives! Satan rules where people take credit for things due God, or give his honor to others.*

If we Christians are to be faithful witnesses to the Lord of lords and King of kings, we must choose a different perspective. We must give him credit and honor for *all* that he has provided and done for us. God is Lord of all and must be praised for all!

Closing (1 minute)

Read aloud Romans 1:24 – 25: "Therefore God gave them over in the sinful desires of their hearts to sexual impurity for the degrading of their bodies with one another. They exchanged the truth of God for a lie, and worshiped and served created things rather than the Creator — who is forever praised."

Pray together and ask God to help you seek meaning and significance from him and him alone. Ask him to forgive you for the times that you have served created things rather than the Creator. Praise him for the life he offers. Thank him for his generous provision. Ask him to open your eyes so you will clearly see Satan's counterfeit offerings for what they are and choose instead to seek God with all your heart, soul, mind, and strength.

Memorize

Therefore God gave them over in the sinful desires of their hearts to sexual impurity for the degrading of their bodies with one another. They exchanged the truth of God for a lie, and worshiped and served created things rather than the Creator — who is forever praised.

Romans 1:24–25

Conquering the Gates of Hell

In-Depth Personal Study Sessions

Day One | The Ongoing Conflict between God and Satan

The Very Words of God

> *Finally, be strong in the Lord and in his mighty power. Put on the full armor of God so that you can take your stand against the devil's schemes. For our struggle is not against flesh and blood, but against the rulers, against the authorities, against the powers of this dark world and against the spiritual forces of evil in the heavenly realms.*
>
> *Ephesians 6:10 – 12*

Bible Discovery

We Have a Role in the Battle between God and Satan

Since before God created the human race, a great battle has taken place between him and Satan. The early Christians realized that the gods of their pagan neighbors were, in fact, counterfeits of Satan designed to deceive them and lure them away from following the true God. In the same way, we also need to recognize Satan's counterfeits and the places in our culture where he exerts his power. Armed with the power of God, we need to take our "stand against the devil's schemes" (Ephesians 6:10–11).

1. What basic conflict is described throughout the Bible, and what are Satan's intentions? (See Genesis 3:1 – 15; Revelation 12:7 – 12, 17.)

2. What is Satan's nature, and what does he try to accomplish?
    (See Genesis 3:1 – 5; Matthew 4:1 – 4; John 8:42 – 47;
    2 Corinthians 11:13 – 15.)

3. In contrast to what Satan wants people to think, who is
    really in charge of this world? (See Ephesians 1:18 – 23;
    1 Timothy 6:13 – 16.)

4. During his ministry on earth, what did Jesus accomplish
    related to the battle between God and Satan, and in what
    ways did he demonstrate his authority and power over
    Satan? (See Matthew 8:28 – 32; 12:22 – 28; Mark 1:21 – 27;
    Hebrews 2:14 – 15.)

5. What role in this battle did Jesus assign to his disciples, and
    in what way(s) did he encourage them? (See Matthew 10:1,
    7 – 8; Luke 10:17 – 20.)

Reflection

Jesus, who has been given all authority in heaven and on earth
(Matthew 28:18), has given those who follow him the authority
"to overcome all the power of the enemy" (Luke 10:19).

Write in your own words a description of the nature, purpose, and significance of the battle between God and Satan.

In what ways do you see Satan at work exerting his power in your world today? Use the chart below as a starting point for learning to recognize the many ways and places in which Satan establishes his throne. (Once you start doing this, you will need much more space!)

Satan at Work	In the world at large	In the communities in which I am involved (work, school, family, etc.)	In my personal life
Presenting a false savior			
Offering counterfeit fulfillment			
Taking credit for what God has done			
Usurping God's authority to define right and wrong			
Creating confusion with false doctrines			

Why is it important for you (and every Christian) to not only recognize the spiritual battle between God and Satan but to know that you have a part in it?

Begin considering the examples of Satan at work that you identified in the chart on page 95 and ask yourself, "What is my role in the battle between God and Satan taking place here? How would God have me take a stand against these schemes of Satan?"

How does knowing God's Word well prepare you to recognize Satan's lies and stand against him?

Who has power over Satan, and how can you appropriate this power in your battle against Satan and his forces?

Memorize

For though we live in the world, we do not wage war as the world does. The weapons we fight with are not the weapons of the world. On the contrary, they have divine power to demolish strongholds. We demolish arguments and every pretension that sets itself up against the knowledge of God, and we take captive every thought to make it obedient to Christ.

2 Corinthians 10:3 – 5

Day Two | Jesus Exposes Satan's Counterfeits

The Very Words of God

> *The coming of the lawless one will be in accordance with the work of Satan displayed in all kinds of counterfeit miracles, signs and wonders, and in every sort of evil that deceives those who are perishing. They perish because they refused to love the truth and so be saved.*

> **2 Thessalonians 2:9 – 10**

Bible Discovery

Jesus Prepared His Disciples Well

Satan has deceived people with his diabolical schemes from the beginning of human history. It is remarkable how closely some of the ancient pagan religions imitated and claimed to provide the same blessings that God provides. Jesus knew what his followers would encounter in pagan cities such as Pergamum, and through his words and actions he prepared them to refute Satan's claims.

DIONYSUS

1. The priests of Dionysus claimed that their god could turn water into wine, but that he did it secretly, at night, in his temple. What was Jesus' first miracle, and when and where did he do it? (See John 2:1 – 11.)

2. Demeter, the goddess of grain, supposedly provided daily
    food for people. Her followers also believed that she offered
    the possibility of resurrection and forgiveness of sins
    through ceremonial washing in the blood of bulls.

    a. In contrast, who did Jesus recognize as the provider of
        all food and nourishment, and what example does the
        text provide of how Jesus' need for these things was
        met? (See Matthew 4:1 – 4, 11.)

    b. In what way did Jesus demonstrate this truth to his dis-
        ciples? (See John 6:1 – 14.)

    c. What did Jesus promise to those who placed their
        faith in him, and in what ways did he demonstrate this
        power? (See John 11:17 – 26, 38 – 44; 20:24 – 31; 1 Corin-
        thians 15:3 – 8.)

    d. How is Jesus able to cleanse people from sin? (See
        Hebrews 9:11 – 14.)

3. Asclepius was known as the god of healing, and people who
    came to him were required to give the god full credit and
    honor for their healing. But what did Jesus do, even for those
    who could not come to him, and how much credit did he
    seek? (See John 4:46 – 53; 5:1 – 13.)

ASCLEPIUS

THINK ABOUT IT

There was a small Asclepius temple in Jerusalem near the Pool of Bethesda. Apparently people believed the myth that the healing powers of Asclepius were at work when the water was moving. That is why the invalid (see John 5:1 – 15) waited beside the pool for thirty-eight years, hoping that he would somehow reach the water and be healed. Certainly people were cured in the Asclepius hospital — by psychological suggestion, demonic powers, and/ or effective medical knowledge of the day. The telltale mark that identifies Asclepius as a diabolical counterfeit is the fact that Asclepius had to be given full credit and honor for any healing that occurred when, in fact, credit is due to the work of God.

4. Followers of Zeus, whose imposing temple could be seen from a great distance, claimed that he was the giver of life, lord of all, and creator of all. How do we know that such claims belong to Jesus alone? (See John 1:1 - 4; 11:25 - 26; Revelation 19:11 - 16.)

DATA FILE
Clever Counterfeits: The False Claims of the Cults

Each of the cults in Pergamum was a counterfeit, a clever copy of the blessings that God alone provides. Each god took credit or honor away from the true God and attributed his blessing to something else—a person, an animal, or an entity of human invention.

Counterfeit Gods	Their Claim(s)	The Truth
Zeus	Acclaimed as king of kings, lord of lords, creator of the universe	God alone is King of kings, Lord of lords, Creator of the universe.
Dionysus	Reputed to provide joy, eternal life, and meaning; said to be able to change water into wine	God alone provides these through Jesus, who turned water into wine and rose from the dead.
Demeter	Said to provide daily bread, redemption, and resurrection to eternal life through the blood of animals	God alone provides these through Jesus, who miraculously fed thousands of people, shed his own blood, and rose from the dead so that people might receive forgiveness for sin and eternal life.
Asclepius	Reputed to provide good health, healing from disease, and eternal life	God alone provides these through Jesus, who healed people, rose from the dead, and provides eternal life.
Emperor Worship	Emperor was viewed as lord of all, the supreme source of truth in the universe	Jesus, seated at God's right hand, is Lord of lords and King of the universe; God is the source of all truth; only he is worthy of worship.
People Today	Give themselves or other things credit for what God has really done (provision, healing, etc.)	People need to have a personal relationship with the one, true God through Jesus the Messiah.

5. The Roman emperor, who declared himself to be the son of a god, lord of all, and the source of truth, demanded to be worshiped as god. In contrast, who does the Bible reveal to be the Son of God, Lord of all, and the source of truth? (See John 1:14; 12:27 – 33; Acts 1:4 – 11; 2:32 – 36.)

Reflection

The people of Pergamum, who lived "where Satan lives" (Revelation 2:13), were surrounded by counterfeits of God's truth. Blinded by the gods of the age, they could not "see the light of the gospel of the glory of Christ" (2 Corinthians 4:4). We, too, are surrounded by a world of enticing counterfeits. Is there a way to discern between the truth of God and the counterfeits of Satan? Is it possible to keep our hearts and eyes open to the light of Christ?

How do *you* know that God is the one true God, the source of all truth, the provider of all blessings, and the giver of eternal life?

Which counterfeits are you equipped to refute by your knowledge of the Word of God?

Which of your personal experiences testify to the truth of God being who he says he is?

How did Jesus' words and actions prepare his disciples to confront and stand firm against Satan's counterfeits?

What effect do Jesus' words and actions have on your willingness and ability to face the strongholds of Satan?

In what way(s) has Satan tried to convince you to believe a counterfeit truth, and how did you respond?

What is at stake when we fall for the trap and believe Satan's lies? What is the impact on us? On people around us? On our witness to a watching world?

Memorize

The god of this age has blinded the minds of unbelievers, so that they cannot see the light of the gospel of the glory of Christ, who is the image of God.

2 Corinthians 4:4

Day Three | Living in the Place Where Satan Lives

The Very Words of God

> *I know where you live — where Satan has his throne. Yet you remain true to my name. You did not renounce your faith in me, even in the days of Antipas, my faithful witness, who was put to death in your city — where Satan lives.*
>
> **Revelation 2:13**

Bible Discovery

Being a Faithful Witness in the Midst of Evil

Satan can be described as living or having his throne wherever he is able to pull people away from God. He accomplishes this by making the pursuit of sin not only acceptable but also appealing and by robbing God of the credit he alone deserves. Believers who live in such places have a great responsibility to remain faithful and true witnesses of God.

1. What are the responsibilities of believers who live in the midst of an evil culture? (See 1 Peter 3:8 – 16.)

2. Each of the following Scripture passages comments on pursuits of evil that were common in the ancient world. Identify the evil pursuit(s) and consider how they were practiced in Pergamum. Then consider the challenges a believer would face in order to be a witness for God in such a culture.

Scripture Text	Evil as Practiced in Pergamum	Maintaining a Witness for God
Lev. 17:10 – 12; Acts 15:19 – 20, 29		

continued on next page . . .

Scripture Text	Evil as Practiced in Pergamum	Maintaining a Witness for God
1 Cor. 6:9–11		
1 Cor. 10:14–21		
2 Peter 2:10–15, 18–19		
1 John 3:7–10		

DATA FILE
Five Candidates for "Satan's Throne"

There are many opinions as to exactly what John referred to when he wrote in Revelation 2:13: "where Satan has his throne" and "where Satan lives." No one knows whether he had in mind a specific temple or pagan practice, or

ALTAR OF ZEUS

whether the sum of the evil activities in Pergamum made the city the home of Satan. In a sense, each of the following pagan centers could be identified as a stronghold of Satan, a place where he had his throne.

The Great Altar of Zeus

Around 250 BC, the people of Pergamum won a great victory against the Galatians. In memory of that event, they built a great altar to Zeus, who was considered to be king of the gods, the life-giver, the lord of all, the creator of all — titles that belong to God alone. Located on the west side of the Acropolis more than one thousand feet above the valley, the altar of Zeus smoked day and night with sacrifices. It could be seen from a great distance and was shaped like an ancient throne. Built on a podium 105 feet by 110 feet, the forty-foot-high altar was the largest in the world. It had three tiers with steps on one side, and each tier had a carved marble frieze featuring scenes of Zeus mythology, which was extremely immoral. Today, the entire altar is in the Pergamum Museum in Berlin.

Dionysus Temple and Cult Center

A beautiful temple dedicated to the god, Dionysus, stood prominently on the Acropolis. The Romans remodeled this small, beautiful temple, which was originally built during the third century before Christ. It was approached by a twenty-five-step stairway at the end of a 770-foot terrace. Here, people worshiped Diony- sus, the fertility god of the vine who was also known as the god of ecstasy, par-

DIONYSUS TEMPLE

ticularly because of the wine he supposedly provided and the orgies related to his worship. During festivals that celebrated him, worshipers consumed

continued on next page . . .

wine in great abundance and gorged on raw meat from Dionysus's sacred animal, the bull, in an effort to be mystically joined to him.

The cult center is believed to have been located on the south side of the Acropolis, near wine shops and a bath house. This center is eighty feet long and thirty-two feet wide. A niche for the idol of Dionysus was positioned to the right of a marble altar. Murals depicting the Dionysus practices were found in frescoes on the low walls around the room. The wine shop next door had several large, baked-clay jars buried in the floor that probably contained wine used in various cultic practices or sold to the public.

Dionysus was considered to be the source of fertility for the grapevines, and one of his symbols was the phallus. He was also viewed as the source of life, so ceremonies dedicated to him included a variety of sexually immoral practices. During festivals, women would drink wine and run through the hills screaming, dancing, and committing sexual immorality. The cult attracted the common people because it promised eternal life to worshipers and catered to human lusts aroused by the pagan cults. Drunkenness and sexual immorality were so extreme during celebrations in Dionysus's honor that for a time his worship was banned in Rome because it was considered too perverse! Again, Satan created a counterfeit to take credit for things of God: eternal life, happiness, purpose, and fertility.

Demeter: The Goddess of Groceries

Believed to be the goddess of grain who provided food, Demeter was popular among common people because acquiring enough food was a dominant concern for them. This secretive cult worshiped in a temple (twenty-two by forty feet) and an 800-seat theater complex on the south side of the Acropolis of Pergamum. It was also known for its death-resurrection theme that focused on Demeter's daughter, who was believed to spend half the year in Hades and the other half on earth. Thus, adherents believed that Demeter offered them the possibility of resurrection.

Although little is known about the rituals of this mystery religion, there was an initiation ceremony involving the blood of a bull. The initiate would stand or lie at the bottom of a pit while a bull was slaughtered above on a grid. The blood would wash over the new convert, providing redemptive cleansing—a clever imitation of salvation through Jesus' shed blood on the cross.

THE POOL IN ASCLEPION

The Cult of Asclepius

Asclepius, the god who was said to heal with moving water, was believed to be the son of the god Apollo and a woman named Coronis. His symbol was the snake, and he was known as the god of life because the snake seemingly resurrects itself (sheds its skin and is born anew, disappears to hibernate and reappears each year). Live snakes were kept in a sacred chest in each of his temples.

Asclepius was also known as "Asclepius Savior," and hospitals or treatment centers were frequently located adjacent to his temples. When the people of Pergamum needed healing, they went to the large Asclepion (hospital) there. In fact, people from all over the world flocked to Pergamum to seek healing. The healing process involved a mixture of religious ceremony and health practices—especially diet, water, herbs, and exercise. Everyone who entered the hospital complex passed a snake symbol and thereby credited any healing they would receive to the snake god.

When patients entered the Asclepion in Pergamum after traveling the kilo-meter-long "sacred way," they were greeted at the gate by temple priests who would interview them to determine their acceptability for healing. Old

continued on next page . . .

people and pregnant women nearing the time of delivery were excluded (no deaths or births were allowed within the sanctuary), as were those who were considered impure. This is an interesting parallel to modern-day cultures that seek to terminate the lives of senior citizens and the unborn.

Each patient who was admitted made an offering (probably incense) to show his or her devotion to Asclepius and began receiving free, supervised treatment. Patients were led through an underground tunnel to a huge treatment room where they went to sleep, probably after being drugged. There they waited to receive a vision of treatment from Asclepius, which they would reveal to the priests, who in turn would prescribe treatment(s). The main treatments related to water, so as part of the healing process patients would take mud baths and drink sacred spring water. Other treatments included special diet, exercise, stress relief, and exposure to the sun.

Any healing that took place—whether as the result of psychological suggestion, demonic powers, and/or the medical knowledge of the day—was credited to Asclepius. Healed people would bow to the statue of Asclepius and the sacred snake to offer thanks, make an offering—apparently a pig—and have their names and the ailments Asclepius had cured inscribed on a marble pillar (usually white). Finally, each healed person would leave a gift with the priests to thank the god and would witness to other people about Asclepius's great ability to heal. Thus many people heard or saw the praise and honor given to Asclepius, which in turn increased the cult's popularity.

Emperor Worship

The center of Roman administration of the province of Asia, Pergamum was also the source and center of emperor worship in the Roman Empire. Julius Caesar was honored with a statue as early as 63 BC. Emperor Augustus was worshiped in the precinct of Athena, and a bronze statue of the emperor (now in the Vatican Museum) was placed there in 31 BC, making Pergamum the first city in the empire to have an emperor cult.

On Caesar Augustus's birthday, the people of Pergamum worshiped him with processions, sacrifices, and a choir singing hymns in his honor. Once a year, everyone in the province was commanded to put incense on the altar of "divine" Caesar and declare, "Caesar is lord." This soon led to significant persecution of Christians, who would not make such a declaration because "Jesus is Lord." They refused to give the emperor honor due to God alone. Possibly the martyr Antipas mentioned in Revelation 2:13 was killed for refusing to worship the emperor. He is the only person besides Jesus who is called a "faithful" or "true" witness in the Bible (Revelation 1:5; 3:14).

Reflection

First Peter 3:15 – 16 outlines the guiding principles for maintaining a witness for God in the midst of evil: "In your hearts set apart Christ as Lord. Always be prepared to give an answer to everyone who asks you to give the reason for the hope that you have. But do this with gentleness and respect, keeping a clear conscience, so that those who speak maliciously against your good behavior in Christ may be ashamed of their slander."

What does it mean for you to set apart Christ as Lord in your heart? Are you doing this? Is there room for improvement?

In what specific ways does establishing Christ as Lord in your heart help you resist the strategies Satan uses to pull you away from God?

What parallels do you see between what you know about the culture of Pergamum and your culture?

Where in your culture would you say Satan lives?

How can you be a "faithful" witness for God in these places? (Review the "Maintaining a Witness for God" portion of the chart on pages 103-104 for specific ideas.)

If someone were to ask you to explain the source of the hope God provides you, what would you say? (If you don't have an answer, perhaps developing one should be a top priority!)

Day Four | Avoiding Every Hint of Sin

The Very Words of God

> *Nevertheless, I have a few things against you: You have people there who hold to the teaching of Balaam, who taught Balak to entice the Israelites to sin by eating food sacrificed to idols and by committing sexual immorality. Likewise, you also have those who hold to the teaching of the Nicolaitans.*
>
> **Revelation 2:14–15**

Bible Discovery

But It's Just Food!

Although God praised the church in Pergamum for its faithfulness in the midst of great evil, he condemned several things that some Christians there were doing. As you explore the following Scripture passages, ask yourself which common activities today are often associated with pagan people and why it is so important for Christians to avoid even the hint of sin.

1. What complaints did God have against some of the Christians in Pergamum, and how seriously did he consider the problem to be? (See Revelation 2:14 – 16.)

2. Why was eating food sacrificed to idols such a significant issue?

   a. In the Old Testament? (See Numbers 25:1 – 3.)

   b. In the New Testament? (See 1 Corinthians 8:4 – 13; 10:18 – 22.)

3. What was so offensive about eating raw meat, meaning meat with blood in it?

   a. In the Old Testament? (See Leviticus 17:10 – 14.)

   b. In the New Testament? (See Acts 15:19 – 20, 28 – 29.)

DID YOU KNOW?

In Revelation 2:15, John's message from God condemned those who followed the teachings of Balaam and the Nicolaitans. Balaam is known for his role in encouraging the Israelites to participate in the feasts and sexual immorality of the Canaanite idols, which led them away from God. Scholars disagree about who the Nicolaitans were. According to church tradition, they comprised a group of people who believed that since they were redeemed by Jesus and, therefore, free in him, they could participate in immoral ceremonies since idols were not gods anyway.

It is interesting to note that both words — *Balaam* (Hebrew) and *Nicolaitans* (Greek) — are derived from words meaning the same thing in their respective languages: "to conquer the people." Biblical writers strongly condemned participation in pagan feasts for many reasons, including the fact that Christians were not to eat meat or drink wine that had been used in sacrifices to pagan gods.

Reflection

Although a Christian is no longer a slave to sin, there is a sense in which we choose to be "slaves" to behavior that honors God. Paul expressed the desire and need for diligence in honoring God in 2 Corinthians 7:1: "Let us purify ourselves from everything that contaminates body and spirit, perfecting holiness out of reverence for God."

What would you say are our cultural equivalents to eating food sacrificed to idols and eating meat with blood in it — activities that are so strongly associated with a pagan worldview or with where Satan lives that a Christian must avoid them "out of reverence for God"?

Make a list of questionable activities that are alluring to us, yet are commonly associated with people who are not Christians.

Are these activities in which you should be participating?
Why or why not?

In what ways might you hinder your witness of God to other
people by participating in these activities?

Which particular activities are condemned by God in his Word,
yet are often practiced by Christians who want to fit into culture?

Are these activities in which you should be participating?
Why or why not?

In what ways might you hinder your witness of God to other
people by participating in these activities?

How sensitive do you believe God wants you to be when it
comes to doing things that could offend other people? How does
this affect what you do and don't do?

Memorize

*Among you there must not be even a hint of sexual immorality, or of any
kind of impurity, or of greed, because these are improper for God's holy
people.*

Ephesians 5:3

Day Five | Standing Stones of the Faith

The Very Words of God

> *As you come to him, the living Stone — rejected by men but chosen by God and precious to him — you also, like living stones, are being built into a spiritual house to be a holy priesthood, offering spiritual sacrifices acceptable to God through Jesus Christ.*
>
> **1 Peter 2:4 – 5**

Bible Discovery

Called to Be Standing Stones

As Christians, our ability to face the future is directly related to our awareness of how God has already worked in our lives. God's work in the past, whether the distant past or our own past, is part of the foundation on which our beliefs and commitment are built. We also have the important responsibility of expressing God's truth to a spiritually hungry world. For both of these reasons, we need to acknowledge and praise God for all that he has done — the ordinary as well as the extraordinary. Thus it is appropriate for God's people to establish "standing stones" as memorials to what he has done.

1. Read each of the following passages and summarize the story or event mentioned, taking note of the work of God that each standing stone commemorates or represents.

Scripture Text	Significance of the "Standing Stone"
Gen. 28:10 – 18	

Josh. 4:1–9	
Josh. 24:19–27	
Rev. 2:12–17	

2. To what does Peter compare believers in 1 Peter 2:4–5?

What kind of life does this require a believer to live?

How does what God is doing reflect the purpose of "standing stones"?

THINK ABOUT IT

Faithful leaders of God's people have always reminded the people to remember what God has done so that they would know what to do and how to live as God desired.

- David encouraged the people to thank God, tell about his wonderful acts, and remember God's wonders, miracles, judgments (1 Chronicles 16:8–12).
- Nehemiah strengthened the resolve of the people by encouraging them to remember the Lord, who is great and awesome (Nehemiah 4:6–14).
- Moses — when instructing the people to care for the widows, aliens, and orphans — told them to remember when they were slaves in Egypt (Deuteronomy 24:17–18, 22).
- Jesus, when helping his disciples understand his miracles, asked, "Don't you remember?" (Matthew 16:5–11; Mark 8:14–20).

Reflection

Using the imagery of the white stones inscribed by people who supposedly had been healed by Asclepius, John challenged believers in Pergamum to stand courageously as witnesses for God.

What are you doing to tell other people what God has done in your life and to give him the credit he is due?

Which aspects of culture and life today stand as obstacles to focusing on God and remembering what he has done?

How might you live differently every day if you had a "standing stone" in your life that helped you *remember* what God has done in your life?

For which specific event — healing, guidance, answered prayer, protection from danger, etc. — might you consider setting up your own "standing stone" as a tribute to God's miraculous work in your life or the life of a loved one?

How do you think people you know — Christians as well as non-Christians — would respond to some kind of "standing stone" in your yard or home? How would you respond?

THE MARK OF THE BEAST

At the beginning of God's message to Christians in Ephesus, the apostle John wrote, "I know your deeds, your hard work and your perseverance.... You have persevered and have endured hardships for my name, and have not grown weary" (Revelation 2:2–3). In light of the challenges early Christians faced in this prominent port city, John's commendation of their faithful testimony for Christ is truly remarkable.

Located on what is now the western coast of Turkey, Ephesus was the crown jewel of Asia Minor. Artistic beauty, cultural learning, erotic pagan worship, world trade, criminal activity, and sorcery flourished amidst great opulence. The city had nearly 250,000 inhabitants and more than twenty pagan temples. Its people enjoyed such luxuries as running water, indoor toilets, beautiful fountains and gardens, colonnaded streets paved with marble, gymnasiums and baths, a library, and a theater that could seat 25,000 people.

The ancient fertility goddess, Artemis, was at the heart of the city's life and economy. Priests guarded and protected the purity of her worship for the entire world, and her temple was one of the seven wonders of the world. Because Artemis was considered to be so powerful and protective of her temple, people from all over the world deposited money there, which the Ephesians loaned out at high rates of interest. Naturally they were very protective of the goddess whom they believed had made them successful, powerful, and rich.

Paul spent time in Ephesus at the end of his second and during his third missionary journeys. Using the Torah, Prophets, and life of Jesus the Messiah, he taught in the local synagogue about the kingdom of God. Later, he went to a lecture hall of Tyrannus, where every day for two years he spoke the good news of Jesus (Acts 19:9 – 10). Paul's clear, fearless presentation of God's truth made a great impact on people. Soon word spread and "all the Jews and Greeks who lived in the province of Asia heard the word of the Lord."

People soon realized that if what Paul and other Christians said was true, Artemis and the other gods of Ephesus were worthless and the city's entire belief system, economy, and lifestyle could collapse. So over time, unless they bore the "mark" of pagan beliefs by living out those beliefs in daily life, the Ephesian Christians faced intense opposition. They became hated second-class citizens who were severely persecuted. Yet the gospel message continued to spread widely because of their bold persistence.

According to tradition, the apostle John came to Ephesus in approximately AD 70. At that time, he was writing or would soon write the book of Revelation, which includes the message to the church at Ephesus mentioned earlier. By this time, the Roman emperor Domitian had gained the upper hand in attracting the Ephesians' religious loyalties. He demanded that people worship him as a god. Even his wife had to address him as "lord" and "god."

The Ephesians built huge structures dedicated to Domitian, including a prominent temple designed to be the world center of Domitian worship. It featured a twenty-seven-foot-tall statue of Domitian that was visible to anyone approaching the city by sea or by land. Altars along the city streets reminded people of Domitian's lordship, and once a year they had to affirm their allegiance to him by saying publicly in front of an altar, "Caesar is lord." Anyone who didn't recognize Domitian's lordship, including Christians who acknowledged the lordship of God alone, was subject to death.

It took passionate commitment and courage for Christians in Ephesus to stand up for their beliefs in the face of the pagan culture in which they lived. One reason they could work tirelessly for Christ is because of the mutual love and support they demonstrated toward one another. Through the love of Jesus, expressed to one another (Revelation 2:4), they could live for him and testify to their world that Jesus is Lord of lords and King of kings.

Opening Thoughts (4 minutes)

The Very Words of God

> *At Iconium Paul and Barnabas went as usual into the Jewish synagogue. There they spoke so effectively that a great number of Jews and Gentiles believed.... So Paul and Barnabas spent considerable time there, speaking boldly for the Lord, who confirmed the message of his grace by enabling them to do miraculous signs and wonders.*

Acts 14:1 – 3

Think About It

It is encouraging when we talk with people about what Jesus has done and they receive it eagerly, but sometimes people are offended when we speak publicly about our faith.

What has been your experience in sharing your Christian beliefs with people who take offense at your beliefs? What did you feel and how did you respond when they challenged your faith?

DVD Teaching Notes (27 minutes)

Ephesus, crown jewel of Asia Minor

Artemis of the Ephesians

Paul begins to teach a message with powerful implications

Who is Lord and God?

A legacy of Christian love

DVD Discussion (6 minutes)

1. Locate Ephesus on the map of Asia Minor on page 123. Why would this city have been important even if it hadn't been the world center for the worship of Artemis and Emperor Domitian?

What was it about this city that enabled Paul and other Christians to make such a significant impact for the gospel?

2. Imagine what it must have been like to live as a Christian in Ephesus. What did it mean for Ephesian Christians to choose who — God, Artemis, or the Roman emperor — they would serve as Lord of their lives?

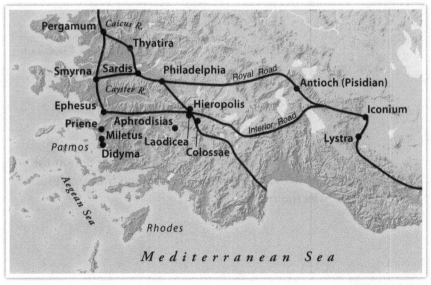

ASIA MINOR

Small Group Bible Discovery and Discussion (13 minutes)

God's Truth Will Make an Impact in Our World

The Word of God is true and powerful. When God's people share its message, it makes an impact. At times, it will turn people's hearts toward God. Other times, it will lead to conflict with people who deny God's truth. Paul and other early Christians experienced both of these responses — and so will we if we tirelessly live out and fearlessly proclaim the truth of God.

1. What happened when Peter shared God's truth with the crowd on the day of Pentecost? (See Acts 2:14 – 21, 36 – 37, 41.)

    What in Peter's message do you think led the people to respond as they did?

2. What happened when Philip preached the news of the kingdom of God in Samaria? (See Acts 8:4 – 13.)

    What response would you have expected from Simon the sorcerer, and what do you think convinced him that Philip's message was the truth?

DID YOU KNOW?
People Will Respond to God's Truth

The Word of God is true, and it *will* make an impact. When early Christian missionaries shared the message of the kingdom of God, some people turned their hearts toward God while others opposed God's truth.

Sharing God's Truth	The People's Response
Peter shared God's truth with the crowd at Pentecost (Acts 2:14–41).	About three thousand people received God's truth and became Christians.
Peter and John healed a beggar and shared the gospel message with people near the temple in Jerusalem (Acts 3–4:4; 4:18–21).	About five thousand men who heard God's truth became Christians. The religious leaders imprisoned Peter and John and ordered them to stop preaching, but they refused. The leaders released them.
Philip preached God's truth to the followers of Simon the sorcerer (Acts 8:9–13).	Simon and many of his followers became believers and were baptized.
Paul and Barnabas preached in Pisidian Antioch to almost the entire city (Acts 13:42–52).	Paul and Silas responded boldly to attacks on their message, and God's Word spread throughout the entire region. Paul and Barnabas were then expelled from the region.
Paul and Silas boldly preached in the Jewish synagogue in Iconium for quite a long time (Acts 14:1–7).	Many Jews and Gentiles became believers, but unbelieving Jews stirred up the people. Upon learning that they were to be killed, Paul and Silas left the city to preach in other places.
After casting an evil spirit out of a girl, Paul and Silas were thrown into prison, but God delivered them. They preached to the jailer and his household (Acts 16:16–34).	The jailer and all his family became believers and were baptized.
Paul spoke to the Corinthians in the house of Titius Justus and taught the Word of God for a year and a half (Acts 18:7–17).	The synagogue ruler in Corinth, his entire household, and many Corinthians became believers. When some Jews took Paul to court, complaining that he was causing people to worship God in unlawful ways, the case was dismissed.

3. What happened when Paul and Barnabas preached in Pisidian Antioch? (See Acts 13:42 – 52.)

What do you think creates a hunger in the hearts of people to hear and receive the Word of God?

Which reasons and emotions, in addition to those mentioned in this passage, often inspire intense opposition to the message of the kingdom of God? Why?

Faith Lesson (4 minutes)

At Iconium, Paul and Barnabas "spoke so effectively that a great number of Jews and Gentiles believed." But as often happens, some people refused to believe. When Paul and Barnabas learned that those who opposed them planned to kill them, they fled in order to continue teaching in nearby cities (Acts 14:1 – 7). God calls us — just as he called the early Christians — to proclaim his Word to our world. He calls us to speak his truth without apology or hesitation and to live out the gospel so that people around us will see and hear the message of God's kingdom.

1. When you have proclaimed the message of God's kingdom in your world, have people received it or opposed it, and how has their response influenced your efforts?

2. To what extent do the words *boldness, courage, passion, fearlessness, faith,* and *perseverance* characterize your public Christian life?

What changes must you make so that these characteristics will be more descriptive of you?

3. What have you learned from the early believers' bold and persistent example that will help you in your efforts to share the truth of the gospel in your everyday world — when other people welcome it as well as when they oppose it?

Closing (1 minute)

Read together Ephesians 6:19 – 20: "Pray also for me, that whenever I open my mouth, words may be given me so that I will fearlessly make known the mystery of the gospel, for which I am an ambassador in chains. Pray that I may declare it fearlessly, as I should."

Considering the opposition he sometimes faced, it is no wonder Paul asked for the prayers of other believers. We need each other's prayers too. Pray together now, asking God to help you boldly, persistently, and tirelessly share the message of Christ. Ask him to fill you with his Spirit so that you may love and support one another as you demonstrate his lordship to a watching world.

Memorize

Pray also for me, that whenever I open my mouth, words may be given me so that I will fearlessly make known the mystery of the gospel, for which I am an ambassador in chains. Pray that I may declare it fearlessly, as I should.

Ephesians 6:19–20

Conquering the Gates of Hell

In-Depth Personal Study Sessions

Day One | Paul's Ministry in Ephesus

The Very Words of God

> *Be very careful, then, how you live — not as unwise but as wise, making the most of every opportunity, because the days are evil. Therefore do not be foolish, but understand what the Lord's will is.*

> **Ephesians 5:15 – 17**

Bible Discovery

God's Truth Bears Fruit in Ephesus

Paul taught in Ephesus longer than in any other location he visited. By learning more about Paul's ministry in Ephesus, we can better understand what the Christians there faced and how God used them to spread his message throughout the world.

1. When Paul arrived in Ephesus, he immediately began seeking out specific people and teaching them about the kingdom of God.

   a. Who were the first people Paul taught? Why would Paul have chosen to teach them, and what did he do for them? What impact might their encounter have had in Ephesus? (See Acts 19:1 – 7.)

b. Which group of people did Paul seek out next and why? What did he teach them? What impact do you think his ministry with them might have had in Ephesus? (See Acts 19:8 – 9.)

c. What was the third group of people Paul taught in Ephesus? Why would Paul have taught there? How much of an impact do we know his teaching had? (See Acts 19:9 – 10.)

d. For how long did Paul teach in Ephesus?

2. The truth of the gospel always undermines the beliefs of paganism. The accounts of Acts 19:11 – 20, 23 – 31 reveal a number of ways in which Paul's teaching was bearing fruit and challenging the status quo in Ephesus.

a. In what ways did Paul's teaching and actions demonstrate God's power over Satan?

b. What impact did this have on the two practices for which Ephesus was famous?

c. List all of the evidence you see that the message of the kingdom of God was changing the lives of people in Ephesus.

DATA FILE
The Theater at Ephesus

In the world of the early Christians, the theater was a significant institution for communicating Hellenism. Every major city in the Roman world had a theater, and the one in Ephesus was spectacular. The Greek king Lysimachus originally built this theater during the third century BC; Emperor Claudius (AD 41–54) enlarged it; and Emperor Nero (AD 54–68) continued renovations.

THEATER AT EPHESUS

These ruins demonstrate how impressive the theater in Ephesus was. It had three tiers of seats and could hold an estimated 25,000 people. The stage was 130 feet wide and 80 feet deep. So imagine how the theater must have

continued on next page . . .

roared when thousands of devotees of the goddess Artemis became angry at Paul and shouted praises to her for two hours!

Although the stage building is mostly gone, it's interesting to note that the audience in Ephesus preferred no backdrop to the stage. They wanted to see life in the city beyond. The drama that took place on the stage portrayed the way the Ephesians viewed themselves; it was a reflection of their lives. In another sense, the drama portrayed the goals for which the culture was striving—who the people wanted to be. So they preferred to see what was happening in their community as a backdrop to what was happening on the stage.

Theaters such as this one were used for entertainment and religious celebrations. Regular plays—dramas (often portraying the myths of the gods), comedies, satires—typically began with sacrifices to Dionysus (the god of theater) and other deities in order to dedicate the presentations to the gods. During a festival honoring a particular god or goddess, a procession would begin at the god's temple and parade through Ephesus. Led by priests and priestesses, the celebrants and pilgrims would carry symbols and statues of their deity. Passersby would honor the god with gifts or by placing incense on altars situated along the route. The procession typically ended at the theater, where the statues were placed on pedestals and worshiped. People then gave speeches, sacrificed animals, and offered the meat on altars in the stage area. Faithful devotees then ate the roasted or boiled meat, symbolizing their communion with the deity.

Thus, it became difficult, if not impossible, for Christians in Ephesus to frequent the theater. They would not participate in pagan sacrifices before dramatic presentations, were offended by stories of gods that the human imagination had created, and refused to eat meat sacrificed to gods that represented demonic powers. No doubt the citizens of Ephesus hated Christians—not so much for their beliefs but for their refusal to compromise and honor the deities that other people worshiped. As emperor worship became more prevalent, Christians risked their lives to avoid such celebrations.

Reflection

The temples of Artemis and other gods were a prominent feature of life in Ephesus. They were a focal point of spiritual life and represented the greatness and power of the gods. An Ephesian probably couldn't imagine a meaningful spiritual life without a temple. Perhaps that's why Paul addressed the Ephesian Christians as "no longer foreigners and aliens, but fellow citizens with God's people and members of God's household" who are being joined together to "become a holy temple in the Lord ... a dwelling in which God lives by his Spirit" (Ephesians 2:19 – 22).

If you had been a Christian in Ephesus, in what ways would the knowledge that God was building you and your fellow believers into a living temple for his glory have encouraged you to proclaim and demonstrate the message of God's kingdom?

In what ways did the temple God was building in Ephesus differ from the temples of the gods of Ephesus, and what life-changing message(s) would it convey to the people who lived there?

As an Ephesian believer, what would you have wanted God's temple to look like and to communicate?

What would that have required of you?

What does being a part of God's living temple require of you today?

PROFILE OF A MAN-MADE GODDESS
Artemis

Who was Artemis?	The supposed goddess of fertility
Who worshiped her?	She was probably the most worshiped deity in Asia and perhaps the world during Paul's time.
What was worship like?	Hundreds of eunuch priests, virgin priestesses, and religious prostitutes served her. Worship rituals were erotic.
By what other names was Artemis known?	"Queen of Heaven," "Savior," and "Mother Goddess"
What role did Ephesus have in Artemis worship?	Ephesus was *neokorus* for Artemis—the world center for Artemis worship and thus responsible for maintaining the cult's purity of worship.
How did Ephesus benefit financially from Artemis worship?	The cult brought great wealth to Ephesus because the temple of Artemis became the world's largest bank during that time.
What were Artemis festivals like?	Devotees came from all over the world to worship and celebrate during her festivals. Huge processions honored her statues. Celebrations were held with music, dancing, singing, dramatic presentations, and chanting of allegiance.
What were Artemis statues like?	They portrayed Artemis as having many breasts—a symbol of her fertility. The main statue in her temple may have been a black meteorite because she was said to have fallen from the sky.
What was the Artemis temple like?	It was one of the seven wonders of the ancient world.
How else do we know that Artemis was important to Ephesus?	Two statues of her have been found in the Prytaneion—the "city hall" of Ephesus, indicating that she was considered to be central to life.
What attracted people to Artemis?	The promise of fertility, long life, sexual fulfillment, and protection during pregnancy and childbirth; the seductive sexuality of her worship

Day Two | Living as Imitators of God

The Very Words of God

> *Be imitators of God, therefore, as dearly loved children and live a life of love,*
> *just as Christ loved us and gave himself up for us as a fragrant offering and*
> *sacrifice to God. But among you there must not be even a hint of sexual*
> *immorality, or of any kind of impurity, or of greed, because these are*
> *improper for God's holy people.*

Ephesians 5:1 – 3

Bible Discovery

Standing Strong in the Power of God

With a population of nearly 250,000 and a reputation for being the richest city in the world, Ephesus was a trend-setting place — not unlike New York City or Los Angeles today. Its seaport, which provided a key link in the Roman world between the east (Persia, Syria, Judea, Egypt) and the west (Greece, Rome), made it a center of political and commercial power. Ephesus was also a stronghold of satanic power: people came from all over the world to worship Artemis; many people were demon possessed; and people practiced magic and sorcery and celebrated emperor worship. Despite these seeming obstacles, the gospel message found fertile ground in this powerful, pagan city where Christians stood for God and refused to acknowledge other deities.

1. Ephesus was a powerful center of evil in the ancient world, but as Paul and the Ephesian believers went about accomplishing God's work, God's power over evil was evident.

    a. How did God demonstrate his power over evil through Paul? (See Acts 19:11 – 12.)

b. How did the name of Jesus come to be respected and honored throughout Ephesus? (See Acts 19:13 – 20.)

2. God's power was evident in Ephesus not only in miraculous and dramatic events, but in the everyday lives of the believers who chose to stand strong for God in the midst of an evil culture. How did Paul instruct the Ephesian believers to live? (See Ephesians 5:8 – 20.)

In what ways would this lifestyle have demonstrated the power of God to people in Ephesus?

DATA FILE
The Sign of the Fish — Ixthus
Early Christians often used the "fish" symbol as an indication of their faith. This may be because Jesus called his disciples to be "fishers of men" (Matthew 4:19). Or, perhaps the Greek word for fish, *ixthus*, was an acrostic for Jesus Christ, Son of God, Savior:

i—first letter in the Greek word for "Jesus"
x—first letter in the Greek word for "Christ"
th—first letter in the Greek word for "God"
u—first letter in the Greek word for "Son"
s—first letter in the Greek word for "Savior"

3. What is the source of a Christian's power to stand firm against evil? (See Ephesians 6:10 – 12.)

How did Paul say the Ephesian believers could appropriate the power to stand their ground? (See Ephesians 6:13 – 20.)

How would each of these items have helped them live as God's holy people in their city?

Reflection

When Paul instructed believers in Ephesus how to be strong in the Lord so that they could stand against evil, he wrote "For our struggle is not against flesh and blood, but against the rulers, against the authorities, against the powers of this dark world and against the spiritual forces of evil in the heavenly realms" (Ephesians 6:12).

Who did Paul say the believers were really fighting as they stood strong for God in Ephesus?

Why is it important for Christians to know who we are really struggling against as we seek to make Christ known in our culture?

What have you seen happen to the witness of Christians when they struggle against "flesh and blood" — against people — in an evil culture rather than against the spiritual forces of evil?

In whose power are you fighting against the powers of evil? Is it working? If not, what changes do you need to make?

Where would you say Satan is most powerful in your culture?

How is God demonstrating his power over evil in this area — through his supernatural acts, through the living witness of Christians?

What is your role in this battle, and to what extent are you living out your part?

THE TRUTH OF THE MATTER
Acknowledging Jesus as Lord

As the early church grew, believers had two choices: (1) to go along with the pagan world in order to not create offense and thus endanger themselves and their families; or (2) to stand firm and declare that Jesus was Lord and risk suffering — even death. The witness of the believers in Ephesus (as well as in cities throughout Asia Minor) was essentially a declaration of war on pagan deities and the Roman state and the satanic foundation on which they were built. The fundamental conflict was between two worldviews competing for world domination, and there could be no compromise.

Today, Christians face a similar choice. Will we totally submit to the lordship of Jesus regardless of the cost? Will we serve him everywhere and in everything, whether the cost is economic, social, or even life itself?

Jesus is Lord. The battle is not between believers and those who do not believe. Rather, it is between Jesus and Satan, and the outcome of that battle has already been determined (see Revelation 20). Our part in the battle as believers is to make Jesus the one and only Lord of our lives and to do it so completely that those who do not yet believe will see the light and abandon their "deeds of darkness."

Memorize

For you were once darkness, but now you are light in the Lord. Live as children of light (for the fruit of the light consists in all goodness, righteousness and truth) and find out what pleases the Lord. Have nothing to do with the fruitless deeds of darkness.

Ephesians 5:8 – 11

Day Three | The Chutzpah Factor

The Very Words of God

> *Some Jews came from Antioch and Iconium and won the crowd over. They stoned Paul and dragged him outside the city, thinking he was dead. But after the disciples had gathered around him, he got up and went back into the city. The next day he and Barnabas left for Derbe. They preached the good news in that city and won a large number of disciples. Then they returned to Lystra, Iconium and Antioch.*

> *Acts 14:19–21*

Bible Discovery

Living out One's Faith with Chutzpah

The apostles persistently taught and lived out Jesus' message because they were totally convinced that Jesus was the Messiah. Jesus also had prepared them well for their task. But they were effective for yet another reason, and it had to do with their understanding of their faith.

In the Jewish culture of that time, the word *faith* had many meanings. One meaning was "bold persistence, unyielding intensity that will not give up," which is the same root for *faith* from which we get the modern Hebrew word *chutzpah*. (It did not mean they were overly pushy, negatively aggressive, or disrespectful toward anyone, which is a connotation that *chutzpah* has in our culture.) We readily see evidence of this Jewish understanding of faith in the ministry of Jesus and in the early Christians who were bold, determined, persistent, and unwilling to be stopped in their service to God.

1. Acting on one's faith with *chutzpah* was nothing new to the people of Jesus' day. How did Abraham demonstrate it in his walk with God? (See Genesis 18:16–33.)

2. What did Jesus teach his disciples about approaching God with *chutzpah*? (See Luke 11:5 - 13; 18:1 - 8.)

3. In what ways did the following people demonstrate *chutzpah* in their pursuit of Jesus, and what was his response?

Scripture Text	Approaching Jesus with Chutzpah
Canaanite woman Matt. 15:21 – 28	
Bleeding woman Mark 5:21 – 34	
Paralytic and his friends Luke 5:17 – 26	
Blind beggar Luke 18:35 – 43	

4. What was the source of boldness for the early Christians, including those in Ephesus? (See Acts 1:8; 4:29 - 31; 2 Timothy 1:6 - 7.)

Reflection

Acts 14:8 – 22 gives an account of Paul's adventurous first visit to
the city of Lystra. Take some time to read this account and see what
you can learn from the ways in which Paul demonstrated *chutzpah* — bold, unwavering, persistent intensity in proclaiming the
news of God's kingdom — in situations that would have caused others to give up.

What did you think as you read about Paul's adventures and saw
the *chutzpah* that characterized his walk with God?

To what extent is your life characterized by bold persistence
and unyielding intensity to do God's will?

If you have known a Christian who is passionate, bold, and persistent in his or her walk with God, what have you learned from
this person about serving God and sharing your faith?

What are people who know you learning from you about living out their faith and serving God? Is it what you want them
to learn?

If you were to pick an area of your life in which you really need to become bolder in your faith, what would it be?

What is the obstacle to demonstrating *chutzpah* in this part of your life, and how willing are you to be bold for Jesus even if it leads to what Paul calls "hardship"?

Memorize

Stand firm. Let nothing move you. Always give yourselves fully to the work of the Lord, because you know that your labor in the Lord is not in vain.

1 Corinthians 15:58

Day Four | Who Will You Worship as Lord?

The Very Words of God

The devil took him to a very high mountain and showed him all the kingdoms of the world and their splendor. "All this I will give you," he said, "if you will bow down and worship me." Jesus said to him, "Away from me, Satan! For it is written: 'Worship the Lord your God, and serve him only.'"

Matthew 4:8 – 10

Bible Discovery

Emperor Worship in Ephesus

Long before the Romans or Paul came to Ephesus, the people of Asia Minor had considered their rulers to be divine. Croesus, king of Sardis (around 550 BC), was honored as a divine king. Alexander the Great declared that he was the divine descendant of Heracles and Zeus. Inhabitants of cities he conquered were delighted to consider him a god and honor him with statues, festivals, and sacrifices. So the people of Asia Minor did not think it unusual when Roman emperors, starting with Caesar Augustus, claimed to be divine.

At the time the early Christians began spreading the gospel message throughout Asia Minor, emperor worship was growing rapidly. Caligula was the first to enforce the worship of emperors. Then Domitian, who was obsessed with his claim to deity, enforced his worship under the threat of death. Ephesians were required to declare him as lord and to sprinkle incense on an altar to indicate their allegiance to him. They were also expected to sacrifice to the emperor and eat sacrificed meat. So Ephesus became quite dangerous for Christians, who believed that no one other than Jesus the Messiah was Lord and, therefore, refused to publicly acknowledge Caesar as lord.

DATA FILE
The Temple of Domitian
Built on the slope of the hill south of Ephesus and extending into the city's center, this prominent temple could be seen from nearly everywhere in Ephesus, including the land and harbor entrances. The Ephesians, who built it to honor their emperor in order to gain the greatest benefits from him, pressured others in the province of Asia Minor to declare the emperor "lord and god."

TEMPLE OF DOMITIAN

Huge columns more than thirty-five feet high supported the 200-by-300-foot podium on which the temple of Domitian rested. One unusual feature is that these columns had carvings that represented various deities. Apparently the Ephesians designed the podium this way in order to declare that the emperor was supported by all the world's gods and that he was the culmination of all deity—the final lord of heaven and earth, the god of gods.

HEAD AND ARM FROM DOMITIAN STATUE

Although the temple itself was not large (forty-by-sixty feet), it had four columns in the front and a row of columns around the outside (eight in front and back, thirteen on the sides). A large, marble altar stood on a raised platform and had a U-shaped colonnade around it with the open end facing the temple. On altars such as this one, the people were required to sprinkle incense to declare that Caesar was lord.

A statue of what is believed to be Domitian stood near the temple and altar. Based on the huge arm and head that have been excavated, researchers believe the statue was twenty-seven feet tall. After Domitian died, he was discredited by the Roman senate, and the temple was rededicated to his beloved father, Vespasian, who was emperor from AD 69–79. Today, the ruins reveal the emperors' great earthly glory and also declare the futility of denying the lordship of the God of the Bible.

1. What event concluded Jesus' final forty days on earth after his resurrection, and why, in light of the growing practice of emperor worship, was it important for Jesus' disciples to witness it? (See Acts 1:1 – 11.)

2. In 1 Timothy 1:3, Paul wrote that he wanted Timothy to stay in Ephesus in order to stand against certain men who taught false doctrine. Based on what Paul emphasized in his final charge to Timothy (1 Timothy 6:11 – 16), what might have been his concern?

3. In what ways does the fact that Roman emperors demanded to be worshiped as "lord" add to the meaning of Romans 10:9 and Philippians 2:5 – 11?

DID YOU KNOW?

A Roman emperor was declared to be divine when a witness came forward claiming to have seen the emperor ascend to heaven or claiming to have seen the emperor's father ascend to heaven (making the current emperor the "son of God"). This process was called *apotheosis*.

4. Why did God strike down King Herod, and how might this event have strengthened the Ephesian believers in their stand against emperor worship? (See Acts 12:21 – 23.)

5. What was Paul's prayer for Ephesian believers, who faced persecution from people who worshiped the Roman emperor and other false gods? (See Ephesians 3:14 – 21.)

Reflection

Worship of the emperor was an integral part of daily life in Ephesus. When an Ephesian saw the impressive Pollio Fountain (built in 93 AD) in Domitian Square or used its abundant fresh water, it was a reminder of the "divine" emperor's generosity in providing life. But believers in Ephesus knew that only Jesus provided water — the living water of eternal life (John 4:7 – 15). So they had to make a choice: to worship the emperor as their provider or to place their faith (and often, their life) on the line and worship Jesus as their provider both for today and for eternity.

In western culture today, people don't commonly throw incense on an altar to show their allegiance to a god or a self-proclaimed divine emperor.

To whom or what do people often show allegiance every day through their words and deeds?

What are some ways (especially subtle ways) in which people worship or declare the lordship of someone or something other than God?

If Jesus is the source of "living water" in your life — the one who gives you life and in whom you place your faith and declare your allegiance, in what ways do you demonstrate your allegiance to him as you go about your daily life?

To what extent do people around you know that you acknowledge Jesus as your provider and worship him as Lord of your life?

In what way(s) have you compromised your allegiance to Christ or marginalized his lordship in your life?

Memorize

You shall not make for yourself an idol in the form of anything in heaven above or on the earth beneath or in the waters below. You shall not bow down to them or worship them; for I, the LORD your God, am a jealous God.

Deuteronomy 5:8 – 9

FACTS TO CONSIDER
The Demands of Emperor Worship

Every person in Ephesus and other cities that worshiped the emperor was expected to:

- Participate in festivals honoring the emperor(s). This included offering incense on altars carried by priests to declare that Caesar was lord, making sacrifices to the emperor, and eating sacrificed meat.
- Offer incense to Caesar before entering the city.
- Obey Caesar without question.
- Acknowledge the emperor's authority when conducting business or shopping in the market. People were to stop at his altars to acknowledge his "lordship" and had to acknowledge the emperor as the provider of life before drawing water from public fountains, etc.

Day Five | First Love

The Very Words of God

> *A new command I give you: Love one another. As I have loved you, so you must love one another. By this all men will know that you are my disciples, if you love one another.*

> *John 13:34–35*

Bible Discovery

Called to Pursue Our "First Love"

Believers in Jesus the Messiah are to love the Lord their God with all their heart, soul, and mind and to love their neighbors as themselves (Matthew 22:37–40). So love for other people is a prominent sign that a person loves God. We know from our study that the believers in Ephesus truly must have loved God in order to remain faithful and obedient to him under the pressure they faced to do evil. Yet over time it seems that their love for one another grew cold.

1. What characterized the Ephesian believers when Paul wrote
    to them, probably around 54 AD? (See Ephesians 1:15 – 16.)

2. Note what characterized the Ephesian believers when John
    wrote to them, probably around 70 AD. (See Revelation
    2:1 – 7.)

    a. For what did John commend them?

    b. For what did John criticize them?

    c. The Ephesian believers had to be very careful to guard
       against the infiltration of evil, false teachers, and theo-
       logical error in their community. How could this have
       led to a loss of love for their fellow believers?

3. How do we know that our love for one another is the evi-
    dence of our love for God? (See 1 John 3:16 – 19, 23 – 24;
    4:7 – 12, 19 – 21.)

4. In his letter to the Ephesians, Paul outlined how the body of
    believers was to be built up in love. Read Ephesians 4:15 – 5:2
    and, using the chart on the next page, note the specific pas-
    sages where Paul addresses the subject. Then write in your
    own words how we are to love one another in the commu-
    nity of believers and the difference it can make.

Scripture Text	What we must do to demonstrate our love	The difference I see this making in my faith community

THINK ABOUT IT
Called to Pursue Our "First Love"

Love distinguishes the community of God's people from people who do not love God. When Paul wrote to the Ephesian believers (probably around AD 54), he mentioned their love for one another (Ephesians 1:15–16) and encouraged loving unity in the body of Christ (Ephesians 4:15–16). Their love for one another is perhaps one reason the church in Ephesus greatly impacted such an evil place. But later, God warned Ephesian Christians that they had forsaken their "first love" (Revelation 2:1–7). This implies that they may have become divided over theological issues.

Unfortunately, many Christians today focus more on their disagreements than they do on loving one another. Could that be one reason the church as a whole is so fractured? Is our lack of love for one another why our witness for Jesus has been greatly weakened? Is it why the Christian community as a whole is not as effective today as it was in Ephesus?

Reflection

Love in action speaks louder than words, but the life of love is a life of tireless sacrifice. Perhaps that is why Paul reminded the Galatians, "Let us not become weary in doing good, for at the proper time we will reap a harvest if we do not give up. Therefore, as we have opportunity, let us do good to all people, especially to those who belong to the family of believers" (Galatians 6:9 – 10).

What is it about the love Christians express toward one another and toward people who do not follow Christ that is such a powerful testimony of God's presence and power, the evidence that God is real and trustworthy?

When (from whom) have you experienced such love in action, and how did it impact your life?

Who in your world do you hope will experience the goodness of God's love as demonstrated by Christian people, and what might be your role in demonstrating such love?

How will you begin loving in a way you have never loved before?

Memorize

Love is patient, love is kind. It does not envy, it does not boast, it is not proud. It is not rude, it is not self-seeking, it is not easily angered, it keeps no record of wrongs. Love does not delight in evil but rejoices with the truth. It always protects, always trusts, always hopes, always perseveres.

1 Corinthians 13:4 – 7

HOT OR COLD

In the book of Revelation, John recorded God's prophetic words to the church in Laodicea: "I know your deeds, that you are neither cold nor hot. I wish you were either one or the other! So, because you are lukewarm — neither hot nor cold — I am about to spit you out of my mouth" (Revelation 3:15 - 16). The geography, and particularly the water sources, of Laodicea and its neighboring cities — Hierapolis and Colossae — provide insight into the meaning of John's message.

Hierapolis, renowned for its healing hot springs, was across the Lycus River Valley about six miles from Laodicea. People with arthritis, skin diseases, and abdominal problems came from distant regions to soak in its warm baths. The gate complex of Hierapolis — two gigantic towers and three arches that opened onto a paved street about a mile and a half long — stands as a testimony to the ancient city's majesty.

The city gates also represented the people's devotion to their deities and rulers. In Hierapolis, the Roman emperor and self-declared god Domitian was worshiped as lord. People who passed through the gates were in a sense acknowledging that Domitian was their god — the provider and protector whom they would honor and obey. Some early believers in Hierapolis were killed because they denied Domitian's authority and declared that Jesus alone is Lord of lords and King of kings. According to ancient church tradition, an early missionary named Philip (most likely the disciple of Jesus from Bethsaida) and his children were brutally executed for this reason. The remains of the Martyrium of Philip still stand on a hill overlooking Hierapolis.

Hierapolis was also the site of the temple of Apollo, god of music, prophecy, and light. In part of the temple, a grand fountain called

Nymphia constantly reminded people that Apollo was their source of life. Next to the temple, a mysterious hole in the ground known as the Plutonium, the Devil's Hole, or the Gates of Hades was believed to be an entrance to the underworld. Poisonous gases emanating from the hole instantly killed any animals that wandered in, but priests of Apollo amazed people by entering the hole and coming out unharmed — seeming to have power over death.

Located about eleven miles from Laodicea, at the foot of Mount Cadmus, Colossae was known for a red dye called *colissinus* and for its invigorating, ice-cold water that streamed down from the snow-covered peak of Mount Cadmus. Colossae was founded several hundred years before Hierapolis and was in serious decline by the time of Paul and John. Christians today know of it because the apostle Paul wrote a letter to the church there.

First-century Laodicea was the richest and most powerful of the three cities. It was known throughout the Roman world for its soft, black wool, healing eye salve, and banking. An ancient writer recorded that this city of about 120,000 people once refused an emperor's offer to rebuild following an earthquake. They apparently told the emperor that they were rich enough and didn't need his money! Despite its prosperity, Laodicea had a serious water problem. Unlike the water of Hierapolis and Colossae, Laodicea's mineral-laden, lukewarm water tasted so bad it made people sick.

In light of the water for which Hierapolis, Laodicea, and Colossae were known, God's message to the church in Laodicea may have meant, "If you were hot, like the springs in Hierapolis, you'd bring healing, restoration, and comfort to suffering people. If you were cold, like the water in Colossae, you'd refresh and encourage hurting people. Instead, you are lukewarm. You don't do anybody any good, and you make me sick — just like your own water." So the challenge for the Christians of Laodicea was to be hot *and* cold — to bring people the healing, refreshing touch of Jesus. It appears they took the warning to heart: the church in Laodicea remained dynamic long after most churches in Asia Minor had disappeared.

Opening Thoughts (4 minutes)

The Very Words of God

> As God's chosen people, holy and dearly loved, clothe yourselves with compassion, kindness, humility, gentleness and patience. Bear with each other and forgive whatever grievances you may have against one another. Forgive as the Lord forgave you. And over all these virtues put on love, which binds them all together in perfect unity.
>
> *Colossians 3:12 – 14*

Think About It

Consider the historic, geographic, or cultural experiences that are common to people in your community — perhaps a natural disaster that people still talk about, a lake that provides economic benefit from fishing and recreation, or longstanding community celebrations that reflect the ethnic heritage of those who settled the area.

How could you use these common experiences to help a nonbeliever in your community understand some aspect of the gospel message or to encourage another believer in his or her walk with God?

DVD Teaching Notes (21 minutes)

Hierapolis

    Its gods

    Its water

Colossae and its water

Laodicea and its water

Changing the world by being hot *and* cold

DVD Discussion (7 minutes)

1. Locate the cities of Laodicea, Hierapolis, and Colossae on the map of Asia Minor and the Lycus River Valley on page 157. Note that Hierapolis is six miles away from Laodicea and is clearly visible across the valley between them. Colossae is eleven miles up the valley from Laodicea.

    What were you surprised to learn about these cities?

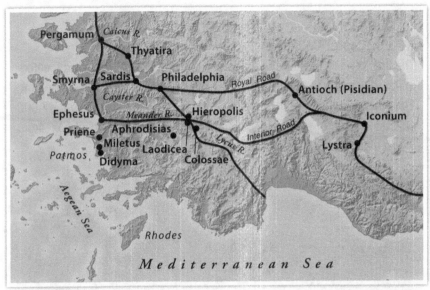

ASIA MINOR

If you had been a Christian living in one of these cities, what daily choices would you have had to make in order to live out and proclaim the gospel message — and change the world of Asia Minor?

2. In what ways does the possibility that a Christian should be both "hot" *and* "cold" change your perspective on what John wrote to the church in Laodicea?

DATA FILE
If This Theater Could Talk

The first-century theater of Hierapolis is one of the best-preserved theaters in Asia Minor. It clearly demonstrates the city's sophistication at the time Epaphras founded a church there. This theater could seat about 17,000 spectators, and in the center of the seating area was a "royal box" from which dignitaries watched events.

THEATER AT HIERAPOLIS

The Greeks and Romans considered the theater to be more than entertainment. The theater was used to display the ideals of the culture and to shape the values and beliefs of those who aspired to be all that a Greek or Roman should be. That's why Greek theaters such as this one were built so that the audience could watch the actors on the stage against the backdrop of their community.

There was also a strong connection between the theater and the worship of pagan gods. Theatrical performances were always dedicated to the gods, and even the architecture of the theater displayed the gods' influence. The remarkably preserved carvings below the stage, which in this theater was twelve feet high, depict the mythology of Apollo and Artemis.

For Christians of that day, the theater created a dilemma. There was nothing inherently sinful about drama, nor did all the presentations insult godly values. However, as an institution, the theater presented a seductive advertisement for a pagan lifestyle.

Small Group Bible Discovery and Discussion (17 minutes)

Called to Be a Healing Influence

God longs for those who follow him to be wholehearted and passionate in presenting his message to a hurting world. Like the water of Colossae, which was cold, fresh, and invigorating, followers of Christ offer a message that refreshes and encourages hearts that are weary of sin. Like the warm, healing mineral waters of Hierapolis, followers of Christ offer a message that brings healing to those who are wounded and broken by sin. And like the nauseating, tepid water of Laodicea, followers of Christ who do nothing — who are neither hot nor cold — turn God's stomach.

1. What is the nature and source of the gift of healing, and why is it given? (See 1 Corinthians 12:4 - 11.)

2. How much power does the Word of God say followers of Jesus have to bring about healing? (See John 14:12 - 14; James 5:13 - 16.)

   To what extent and in what ways do God's people exercise this gift and power in the world today?

How much responsibility do you believe God has given to the Christian community to care for people who are suffering?

3. Matthew 25:34 – 40 mentions six types of healing in which Christians are to be involved. What are they?

In what specific, practical ways can your faith community reach out to people with each of these unmet needs and be healing "hot" water and/or refreshing "cold" water?

NOTE: Take some time to come up with ideas that would meet deep needs in your community. Options may include helping in a food pantry, providing winter coats for the children of prison inmates, helping a refugee family get established in a new community, etc.

4. What kind of healing can Christians offer that other people often do not, and where do you think this is most needed — in your local community and in our world? (See Colossians 3:13.)

Faith Lesson (5 minutes)

In a letter to the Corinthians, Paul describes God as "the Father of compassion and the God of all comfort, who comforts us in all our troubles, so that we can comfort those in any trouble with the comfort we ourselves have received from God" (2 Corinthians 1:3 – 4). Many Christians today, however, are too consumed by the busyness of our own lives to be responsive to how God wants us to be a healing influence in our world. Yet God has not changed. He is still the "Father of compassion and the God of all comfort," and he longs for us to share the healing comfort of his love in our needy, hurting world.

1. In what way(s) has God comforted you when you have been hurting or in need? Imagine what it would mean to share that comfort with a hurting person who otherwise might not receive it.

2. In terms of being a healing influence in the world, what's your temperature — hot? cold? tepid?

3. In which practical ways can you be more like "hot" water, bringing healing and comfort to hurting people? To which specific individuals?

4. In which practical ways can you be more like "cold" water, sharing encouragement through the caring love of Jesus the Messiah? To which specific individuals?

Closing (1 minute)

Think of it! God wants to use you and me to be *hot* or *cold* wherever we are so that people who are hurting and needy will see a glimpse of his kingdom and be drawn into a personal relationship with him. Read together Colossians 3:12: "As God's chosen people, holy and dearly loved, clothe yourselves with compassion, kindness, humility, gentleness and patience," and go out into your world and influence your culture for God.

Ask God to help you be a healing and invigorating influence for his glory every day. God longs to renew you every day and guide you by his Spirit to people who need his healing touch. Ask him to strengthen your commitment to regular prayer and Bible study so that you will be equipped to do his works of service. Ask for the humility and servant's heart to be the loving hands of Jesus to those who are in need.

Memorize

As God's chosen people, holy and dearly loved, clothe yourselves with compassion, kindness, humility, gentleness and patience.

Colossians 3:12

Conquering the Gates of Hell

In-Depth Personal Study Sessions

Day One | Thirsty for Living Water

The Very Words of God

> *O God, you are my God, earnestly I seek you; my soul thirsts for you, my body longs for you, in a dry and weary land where there is no water.*
>
> **Psalm 63:1**

Bible Discovery

Come to Me and Drink

In the Word of God, imagery of water is used frequently to convey a spiritual message. The message of Revelation 3, for example, hinges on the imagery of the refreshing, ice-cold water of Colossae; the warm, healing water of Hierapolis; and the foul-tasting, lukewarm water of Laodicea. As you study the following passages, keep in mind the invigorating, free-flowing streams of Colossae. They are an appropriate image of the "living water" of God, a gift that followers of Jesus are called to offer to others.

1. David's psalms are known for their vivid descriptions of our human longing for God. Note the ways in which David expressed his desire for God in Psalms 42:1 – 2 and 63:1 – 8. How would you describe your need for God?

2. What amazing promise does God make to spiritually thirsty people who search for him? (See Isaiah 41:17 – 20.)

Why does God do these things?

How closely do the waters of Colossae fit this description, and in what way does this promise help you better understand John's message in Revelation 3?

3. How did the Samaritan woman respond when Jesus told her about the living water he could provide? (See John 4:10 - 15; also 4:16 - 42.)

   What do you think she was hoping for, and what did she find? (John 4:25 - 26, 28 - 30.)

4. What did Jesus promise to people in Jerusalem, and what did John say "living water" symbolized? (See John 7:37 - 39.)

DID YOU KNOW?

For people in ancient times, "living water" (Hebrew: *mayim chayyim*) was fresh and free-flowing, like water from a spring or stream. It was not water that had been drawn from a well or cistern, nor was it water that had been put into a container and carried from its source.

STREAM OF "LIVING WATER" IN COLOSSAE

5. In Isaiah 32:1 – 2, which images are used to describe people who stand for righteousness and justice — those who drink the living water of God?

   What do you learn about what God's people are called to be from these descriptions?

Reflection

God alone can satisfy our human need for living water, but many of us insist on seeking it in our own ways. As a result, we wander in a "parched land" — hungry, thirsty, and needy. But God's love and care for us cannot be quenched, and he will supply living water in abundance to everyone who accepts him as Lord.

Take a few moments to read Psalm 107:1 – 9, 35 – 36.

What does this psalm say to you about what God wants to do in your life?

What does this psalm say to you about what God has called you to do in the life of a person who is thirsty, hungry, and in need of his living water?

Memorize

Whoever drinks the water I give him will never thirst. Indeed, the water I give him will become in him a spring of water welling up to eternal life.

John 4:14

Day Two | The Church in Colossae

The Very Words of God

> *We always thank God, the Father of our Lord Jesus Christ, when we pray for you, because we have heard of your faith in Christ Jesus and of the love you have for all the saints — the faith and love that spring from the hope that is stored up for you in heaven.... All over the world this gospel is bearing fruit and growing, just as it has been doing among you since the day you heard it and understood God's grace in all its truth.*

Colossians 1:3–6

Bible Discovery

A Church Overflowing with God's Love

Colossae, at the foot of Mount Cadmus, was a city in decline by the time the gospel message came to Asia Minor. Although the nearby cities of Laodicea and Hierapolis had grown more prominent and prosperous than Colossae, the reputation of its cold, fresh, rushing water was still widely known. It seems that the city was also known for its vibrant, loving Christian community.

1. How had the people in Colossae learned about the kingdom of God? (See Acts 19:8–10; Colossians 1:3–8.)

2. How well did Paul know the Colossian believers, and how much did he care for them? (See Colossians 2:1–5.)

3. What had Paul heard about Philemon, a leader of the church in Colossae? (See Philemon 4–7.)

In what way were Philemon and, we assume, other believers being "cold" water in their world?

What impact did their faithful service to Christ have on Paul?

4. What did Paul specifically ask Philemon to do? (See Philemon 10 – 22.)

What did Paul expect the outcome of his request to be, and how would it be yet another example of believers offering a "cup" of cold, refreshing water and thereby influencing their world for God?

5. According to Colossians 2:8, 16 – 23, what challenges was the church facing?

How do you think these challenges would have affected their love for one another and their ability to share the refreshing, living water of God in their world?

PROFILE OF A CITY
Colossae

Located in the fertile Lycus River Valley on the trade routes between Persia and the port city of Ephesus, Colossae was an important commercial center during the fifth century BC. By the time of the early church in the first century AD, however, Hierapolis and Laodicea had eclipsed Colossae in importance and its population had diminished to about fifty thousand.

The city was widely known for three things:

- Its cloth and a brilliant red dye called *colossinus*
- Its streams of fresh, ice-cold water fed by the snow-capped mountains that towered above it
- Its agriculture made possible by the fertile soil of the Lycus River Valley irrigated by mountain-fed streams

Inhabitants of Colossae worshiped many gods, including Zeus, Artemis, Athena, and Demeter—in part because of the area's agricultural fertility, which ancient people often attributed to the favor of the gods. There was also a large Jewish population—perhaps as many as ten thousand people—which may be part of the reason Christianity spread rapidly.

In AD 60, the city was almost completely destroyed by an earthquake and was gradually abandoned.

Reflection

When Paul wrote to the Colossians, he had heard of their vibrant faith and love for one another. After addressing the problem of deceptive philosophies that could have created division and quenched the testimony of their love for one another, Paul instructed them how to live so that their love would remain strong and the name of God would be glorified.

Paul's instructions are no less important for Christians today who want to live out a life of faith and demonstrate God's love to a hurting world. After you read Colossians 3:1 – 17, use the following questions to take a personal inventory of steps you need to take in order to become the refreshing, cold water God has called you to be.

What threatens to distract the focus of your heart and mind from Christ and his kingdom?

Which characteristics and practices of your earthly nature do you need to put to death so that you may walk in the new life God has given you?

In your relationships with people both inside and outside your community of faith, what do you need the most — compassion? kindness? humility? gentleness? patience?

Which people or grievances are most difficult for you to forgive?

What forgiveness do you need to give or receive in order to restore your relationship with another member of the body of Christ?

What are you doing to ensure that the word of Christ will "dwell in you richly" and be reflected in all of your words and deeds?

Memorize

Just as you received Christ Jesus as Lord, continue to live in him, rooted and built up in him, strengthened in the faith as you were taught, and overflowing with thankfulness.

Colossians 2:6 – 7

Day Three | A Light Shining in the Darkness

The Very Words of God

The god of this age has blinded the minds of unbelievers, so that they cannot see the light of the gospel of the glory of Christ, who is the image of God. For we do not preach ourselves, but Jesus Christ as Lord, and ourselves as your servants for Jesus' sake. For God, who said, "Let light shine out of darkness," made his light shine in our hearts to give us the light of the knowledge of the glory of God in the face of Christ.

2 Corinthians 4:4 – 6

Bible Discovery

Let His Light Shine in Our Hearts

Light and darkness held great meaning for people in the ancient world, and gods of light were honored greatly. Perhaps one reason the apostle John used the concept of "light" more than thirty times when writing to the church in Asia Minor is because the god Apollo was, among other things, considered to be the god of light. So notice how God, through the inspired writers, communicated his message of light and life to the people of Asia Minor.

1. Describing the God of Israel as a light that dispels darkness was not a new concept for those who spread the news of God's kingdom in Asia Minor. As you read the following passages, note how images of light are used to describe God and his gift of salvation. (See 2 Samuel 22:29; Psalms 27:1; 89:15.)

What imagery did Isaiah use when he predicted the coming of the Messiah? (See Isaiah 9:2.)

2. What did Paul urge the Christians of Colossae to do because of what God had done for them? (See Colossians 1:10 – 14.)

If they had not personally visited the Apollo temple and "Gates of Hades" in Hierapolis, the Christians of Colossae certainly had heard about them and seen the temple from a distance. Considering their proximity to the darkness of the underworld and their knowledge of Apollo, a supposed god of light, what do you think they thought when they read Paul's description of what God had done for them? (See Colossians 1:12 – 14.)

3. Which images did Paul use to help the Ephesian Christians understand their new identity as children of God? List as many as you can. (See Ephesians 5:8 – 14.)

In what ways do you think these images helped Christians discern how to live lives that would please the Lord?

4. Keeping in mind that Apollo was considered the god of light, how do you think his followers would have responded to what Jesus said about himself in John 8:12?

5. What do you think it meant to the disciples when Jesus told them that they were "the light of the world"? (See Matthew 5:14–16.)

    How had they seen Jesus demonstrate that he was the light of the world?

    In what specific ways had Jesus let his "light shine before men" that they saw his good deeds and praised his Father in heaven?

    How might Jesus' example have encouraged believers in Hierapolis to be bold witnesses of God's kingdom to followers of Apollo?

DATA FILE
The Temple of Apollo in Hierapolis

Located on the main street between the theater and a sacred pool, the entrance to this forty-by-sixty-foot temple was approached by a broad flight of stairs. A row of six columns graced the front of the temple, and to the left of the stairs a large public fountain brought fresh water—compliments of Apollo, the giver of life—into the city.

The Temple of Apollo was actually built above the Plutonium, the cave that people believed led to the underworld. Pluto (or Hades, as the Greeks called him) was viewed as the god of the underworld and supposedly came and went via the cave opening next to the temple.

TEMPLE OF APOLLO

The Plutonium played an important role in the culture of that day. Strabo, a Roman writer, described the fenced plaza in front of the misty cave opening where ceremonies took place. No doubt the consequences of entering the cave had much to do with its importance. All living, breathing things—animals, birds, people—except the priests of Apollo, died instantly if they entered it and breathed its poisonous gases. No one knows how the priests survived. Perhaps they held their breath or had an unknown source of fresh air. Even today poisonous gases seep out of the cave, so its entrance is blocked by a fence to protect the unwary.

Reflection

The human heart longs for true light and life, which are found only in the God of Israel, the God of light in whom there is no darkness (1 John 1:5). Jesus, the Son of God, assures those who follow him that they "will never walk in darkness, but will have the light of life" (John 8:12). As believers, we belong to God and have been called to let the light of God shine as we "declare the praises of him who called you out of darkness into his wonderful light" (1 Peter 2:9).

In what ways has God turned your spiritual darkness into light?

How much do you appreciate and express your gratitude for what God has done?

What do you think Paul meant when he encouraged the Ephesians to live as "children of light," and what does living this way require in your world?

How do you go about learning what pleases the Lord?

When God exposes sinful and fruitless "deeds of darkness" in your life, how do you respond?

Think about your day-to-day life. To what extent are you truly living in the light of Christ, and to what extent do you choose to live in darkness? How will those around you see the light of God if you do not live fully in his light?

Day Four | Being a Totally Committed Witness of Christ

The Very Words of God

Now I rejoice in what was suffered for you, and I fill up in my flesh what is still lacking in regard to Christ's afflictions, for the sake of his body, which is the church. I have become its servant by the commission God gave me to present to you the word of God in its fullness.... We proclaim him, admonishing and teaching everyone with all wisdom, so that we may present everyone perfect in Christ.

Colossians 1:25 – 28

Bible Discovery

Faithful Talmidim

As *talmidim,* the disciples of Jesus were passionately committed to living life as he did — to walk as he walked and, by doing so, to show people what the kingdom of God was like. Using what Jesus had taught them, or what they had learned through other believers, the disciples of Jesus and early Christians passionately proclaimed the gospel throughout the Roman world. They were prepared and committed to respond to the opportunities God provided to witness for him. Based on church history, it appears that Jesus' disciple Philip, from the small town of Bethsaida, was God's messenger in Hierapolis. According to the Bible, another determined follower of Jesus, Epaphras, probably founded the churches of Laodicea, Hierapolis, and Colossae. God used these men and other believers like them to change their world. Christians today have no less of an opportunity to live as Jesus' faithful *talmidim* and bring his message of salvation to a lost and hurting world.

1. What do the following verses reveal about Philip's commitment to being a *talmid* of Jesus?

Scripture Text	Philip, talmid of Jesus the rabbi
Mark 3:13–19	
John 1:43–49	
John 12:20–22	

2. Read John 6:1–14 and 14:6–14. In what ways would these two situations have expanded Philip's vision and prepared him for his later ministry in a Gentile world?

3. What do the following passages reveal about Epaphras and his faithful, tireless work on behalf of the gospel?

Scripture Text	Epaphras, faithful messenger of the gospel
Col. 1:1–8	
Col. 4:12–13	
Philem. 23	

Reflection

Philip and Epaphras were two *talmidim* who were totally commit-ted to obeying Jesus' commands and walking as he walked (1 John 2:3 – 6). In the Lycus River Valley, their walk with him changed the world so dramatically that two thousand years later, long after the great cities in which they ministered have turned to ruins, we still know about their faithful witness for God.

What would it take for you to be as passionate and determined a follower of Jesus as Philip and Epaphras?

Which sacrifices or changes in priorities might you need to make?

What may be holding you back from actively living out your faith in your world and showing people the healing and hope of the kingdom of God?

Do you really believe that God can use you to change the world — for another person, for families, for your community, for your country? Why or why not?

As you look at the world in which you live, identify where the life-changing power of the kingdom of God is most needed. Ask God to prepare you, give you an opportunity, and show you how to make an impact for his kingdom.

Identify some aspect of your faith — your knowledge of
God's Word, how God has changed your life, your walk with
God — that you can share with others. Ask God to help you to be
more faithful and bold in sharing this news with your world.

THE TRUTH OF THE MATTER
Confronting the Hellenism of Our World

"Man," said the Greek philosopher Protagoras (481 – 411 BC), "is the measure of all things of what is and what is not." This philosophy provided the foundation for Hellenism, which was devoted to the supremacy of human beings and human accomplishment. The cultural tradition of the Greeks, Hellenism was the prevalent worldview before and during the growth of early Christianity.

Hellenism was based on the belief that human beings are the ultimate source of truth and authority in the universe. Truth is defined as that which each person can logically understand and demonstrate (or at least that which the majority of people decides is right). Since the human being was considered the "measure of all," human wisdom was deemed to be the greatest wisdom. What could not be understood or explained was viewed as false. Human accomplishments in athletics, the arts, and architecture became the motivating drive of society. The human body was considered the ultimate in beauty, so nudity in art, in the baths, and in sport was common. The accumulation of material possessions in order to provide oneself with luxury and comfort was a common pursuit. What could be more natural than to get the most out of life? After all, life's greatest goal was to be the best at any pursuit.

Hellenists tried to build their society on their gods, which were human creations. In effect, they worshiped themselves. Because they had nothing greater than themselves on which to base their worldview and society, their

continued on next page . . .

society eventually collapsed. No society can exist for long when it creates its own view of truth.

Was Hellenism, at its roots, really new? No. The first evidence of it is recorded in Genesis 3:1 when Satan asked Eve, "Did God really say ... ?" Eve, and then Adam, faced an earth-shaking choice: who, or what, was the ultimate source of truth in the universe? In deciding to disobey God's command about eating fruit from the tree (Genesis 2:16 – 17), Adam and Eve decided for themselves what was right and best for them and didn't depend on God. They crowned themselves as the ultimate authority in the universe.

In contrast, the worldview of Christianity is based on God as the ultimate truth and authority. His revelation is the source of our vision for society, our knowledge, our morality, and even truth itself. The resulting values are absolute — not merely creations of our imaginations — and form a strong basis for society and the belief in the dignity of each person who is created in God's image. In such a worldview, God is the ultimate authority in the universe. Life is to be lived for him, not for ourselves. God, not humankind, has created the ultimate in beauty. Truth is what God has revealed and allowed people to discover.

Hellenism's core beliefs haven't disappeared with today's cultural advancements. Today Hellenism goes by other names — Humanism, or its contemporary expression, Postmodernism — and still promotes the idea that the human being is the ultimate authority in the universe. Thus truth is what the human mind can discover, demonstrate, and understand. The glorification of human accomplishment, the drive to be number one, the obsession with comfort and pleasure, the focus on the human body and sexuality, the lack of compassion for people, and the commitment to the will of the majority as being right are built on a foundation that is as old as the garden of Eden and was well articulated by ancient Greek philosophers.

The signs of Hellenism are evident in catch phrases we hear every day: "Just do it." "If it feels good, who can tell you it's wrong for you?" "You can accomplish anything you set your mind to do." "I have the right to choose what to do with my body." And the Hellenistic perspective is the dominant paradigm within our public education system.

What does this mean for Christians today? We live in a world that is similar in how it views life and spiritual truth to the world in which the early Christian missionaries lived. Our great task is to proclaim the truth about God and his kingdom and to demonstrate the life-giving power of that kingdom through our obedience to God's commands. Our great temptation is that we may compromise and live as Hellenists or Humanists — and lose the opportunity to bring God's life-transforming light and truth to our spiritually needy world.

Day Five | Challenged to Be Hot or Cold

The Very Words of God

I know your deeds, that you are neither cold nor hot. I wish you were either one or the other! So, because you are lukewarm — neither hot nor cold — I am about to spit you out of my mouth.

Revelation 3:15 – 16

Bible Discovery

Images That Convey an Urgent Message

God's inspired Word speaks to all people. Although we can understand the Bible without knowing the cultural settings in which particular books were written, we can learn even more by learning the common images and symbols the biblical writers used. The apostle John, for example, used a number of metaphors from history, culture, and geography in his Revelation 3 letter to the church in Laodicea. He used images of the Laodiceans' everyday world in order to more effectively communicate the importance and urgency of God's message.

Read Revelation 3:14 – 19. For each of the images John used, first identify what it may have referred to and then consider what it would have meant to the people of Laodicea. (You may need to review some of the "Data Files" in previous studies to understand all of the images.)

Image Used	What this image may have referred to and meant to the Christians of Laodicea	What this image says to me about my witness in the world
You are neither cold		
... nor hot		
Because you are lukewarm		
I am about to spit you out of my mouth		
You say, "I am rich; I have acquired wealth and do not need a thing"		
But you do not realize you are wretched, pitiful, poor, blind and naked		
I counsel you to buy from me gold refined in the fire		
Buy from me white clothes to wear		
Buy from me salve to put on your eyes, so you can see		

DID YOU KNOW?
What Happened to the Church in Laodicea?
Church history records that the church in Laodicea remained dynamic after most churches in Asia Minor disappeared. One of its bishops was martyred for his faith in AD 161, long after John wrote his warning to the city in the book of Revelation. In AD 363, Laodicea was the location chosen for a significant church council. So, it appears that the church in Laodicea learned its lesson, and God continued to bless the Christian community there for some time.

Reflection

The images John used to convey God's message to the church in Laodicea convey a message to Christians today as well. Look again at each of the images John used and give some thought as to what God's message to the Christians in Laodicea means to you — your walk with God and your witness in the world. Consider specific situations where you can make a difference, specific attitudes that hinder communication of God's message, and positive actions you can take.

If you were to describe a type of water that symbolizes your walk with God right now, would it be a fast-flowing mountain stream? a clear, sparkling pool? a warm bath? a thundering waterfall? a stagnant pool? Why?

If your answer is not what you would like it to be, what are you going to do about it?

DATA FILE
Laodicea
History

The most prominent city in the Lycus River Valley during the first century, Laodicea was destroyed by an earthquake in AD 60. According to the Roman writer Tacitus, Rome offered to pay for the city to be rebuilt, but the people declined, saying that they were wealthy enough to restore their own city.

Industry

The city was renowned for three main industries:

- A banking center for the province of Asia Minor, including a gold exchange
- The textile center where glossy, black wool was woven into garments called *trimata* that were prized in the Roman world
- The location of a major medical school known worldwide and where an eye salve called Phyrigian powder was made from a local stone

Geography

Although it was located in the fertile Lycus River Valley, the city had no nearby water source. Mineral-laden water was piped in from six miles away. By the time it reached the city, it was lukewarm and, because of the high mineral content, was nauseating enough to actually make people sick.

ENCRUSTED STONE WATER PIPES OF LAODICEA

Which commonly understood images of culture are you able to use in communicating God's message to spiritually needy people?

In which specific ways might you use your background, training, and/or interests to better communicate the message of Jesus to your world?

Memorize

Whatever you do, whether in word or deed, do it all in the name of the Lord Jesus, giving thanks to God the Father through him.

Colossians 3:17

TIMELINE OF EVENTS IN AND AROUND ASIA MINOR

Date(s)	Event
2000–1000 BC	Hittite Empire
920–586 BC	Divided kingdom of Israel
586 BC	Babylonian captivity
500 BC	Jews' return from captivity
325 BC	Alexander the Great's conquest
261 BC	Laodicea founded
220 BC	Antiochus settles Jews from Babylon in Asia
133 BC	Roman Empire begins; lasts until AD 300
27 BC–AD 14	Caesar Augustus's rule
AD 37–41	Caligula's rule (enforced emperor worship)
c. AD 46–57	Paul's missionary journeys
c. AD 60	Paul is martyred
AD 60	Earthquake damages Laodicea, Hierapolis, and Colossae
c. AD 68–78	The apostle John is in Asia
AD 81–96	Domitian's rule/emperor worship in Ephesus
AD 90–100	John writes the book of Revelation
AD 98–117	Emperor Trajan rules
c. AD 110	John's death
c. AD 325	Christianity becomes the state religion
AD 363	A significant church council is held in Laodicea

BIBLIOGRAPHY

To learn more about the cultural and geographical background of the Bible, consult the following resources:

Akurgal, Ekrem. *Ancient Civilizations and Ruins of Turkey*. Istanbul: Haset Kitabevi, 1985.

Barclay, William. *The Revelation of John*. Philadelphia: Westminster Press, 1960.

Beitzel, Barry J. *Moody Bible Atlas of Bible Lands*. Chicago: Moody Press, 1993.

Bivin, David. *Understanding the Difficult Words of Jesus*. Shippensburg, Pa.: Destiny Image Publishers, 1994.

Butler, Trent C., ed. *Holman Bible Dictionary*. Nashville: Holman Bible Publishers, 1991.

Crawford, John S. "Multiculturalism at Sardis." *Biblical Archaeology Review* (Sept. – Oct. 1996).

De Vries, LaMoine F. *Cities of the Biblical World*. Peabody, Mass.: Hendrickson, 1997.

Edmonds, Anna G. *Turkey's Religious Sites*. Istanbul: Damko, 1997.

Friesen, Steven. "Ephesus: Key to a Vision in Revelation," *Biblical Archaeological Review* (May – June 1993).

Hamilton, Edith. *Mythology*. New York: Penguin Books, 1969.

Safrai, Shmuel, M. Stern, D. Flusser, and W. C. Van Unnik.*The Jewish People in the First Century*. 9 vols. Amsterdam: Van Gorcum, 1974.

Visalli, Gayla. *After Jesus: The Triumph of Christianity*. New York: Reader's Digest, 1992.

Ward, Kaari. *Jesus and His Times*. New York: Reader's Digest, 1987.

Yamauchi, Edwin. *The Archaeology of New Testament Cities in Western Asia Minor*. Grand Rapids, Mich.: Baker, 1980.

Young, Brad. *Jesus the Jewish Theologian*. Peabody, Mass.: Hendrickson, 1995.

———. *Paul the Jewish Theologian*. Peabody, Mass.: Hendrickson, 1999.

More Great Resources
from Focus on the Family®

Volume 1: Promised Land

This volume focuses on the Old Testament—particularly on the nation of ancient Israel, God's purpose for His people, and why He placed them in the Promised Land.

Volume 2: Prophets and Kings of Israel

This volume looks into the nation of Israel during Old Testament times to understand how the people struggled with the call of God to be a seperate and holy nation.

Volume 3: Life and Ministry of the Messiah

This volume explores the life and teaching ministry of Jesus. Discover new insights about the Son of God.

Volume 4: Death and Resurrection of the Messiah

Witness the passion of the Messiah as He resolutely sets His face toward Jerusalem to suffer and die for His bride. Discover the thrill the disciples felt when they learned of His resurrection and were later filled with the Holy Spirit.

Volume 5: Early Church

Capture the fire of the early church in this fifth set of That the World May Know® film series. See how the first Christians lived out their faith with a passion that literally changed the world.

Volume 6: In the Dust of the Rabbi

"Follow the rabbi, drink in his words, and be covered with the dust of his feet," says the ancient Jewish proverb. Come discover how to follow Jesus as you walk with teacher and historian Ray Vander Laan through the breathtaking terrains of Israel and Turkey and explore what it really means to be a disciple.

Volume 7: Walk as Jesus Walked

Journey to Israel where the 12 disciples walked the walk their rabbi Jesus taught them. Examining the culture and the politics of the first century. Ray Vander Laan opens up the Gospels as never before.

FOR MORE INFORMATION

Online:
Go to ThatTheWorldMayKnow.com

Phone:
Call toll-free: 800-A-FAMILY (232-6459)
In Canada, call toll-free: 800-661-9800

More Great Resources
from Focus on the Family®

Volume 8: God Heard Their Cry

Just when it seemed that Pharaoh could not be defeated, God provided for His People in ways they never could have imagined. Join historian Ray Vander Laan in ancient Egypt for his study of God's faithfulness to the Israelites—and promise that remains true today.

Volume 9: Fire on the Mountain

When the Israelites left Egypt, they were finally free. Free from persecution, free from oppression, and free to worship their own God. But with that freedom comes a new challenge—learning how to live together the way God intends. In this ninth set of That the World May Know® film series, discover how God teaches the Israelites what it means to be part of a community that loves Him, and the lessons we can begin to live out in our lives today.

Volume 10: With All Your Heart

Do you remember where your blessings come from? In Exodus, God warned Israel to remember Him when they left the dry desert and reached the fertile fields of the promised land. But in this tenth volume of That the World May Know® film series, discover how quickly the Israelites forgot God and began to rely on themselves.

Volume 11: The Path to the Cross

Discover how the Israelites' passionate faith prepares the way for Jesus and His ultimate act of obedience and sacrifice at the cross. Then, be challenged in your own life to live as they did by every word that comes from the mouth of God.

Volume 12: Walking With God in the Desert

Are you going through a difficult period of life? The loss of a loved one? Unemployment? A crisis of faith? During these desert times, it's easy to think God has disappeared. Instead, discover that it's only when we are totally dependent on Him that we find Him closer than ever and can experience God's amazing grace and provision.